THE FUTURE
OF THE UNIVERSE

THE
FUTURE
OF THE
UNIVERSE

Chance,
Chaos, God?

ARNOLD
BENZ

Continuum
New York   London

2000

The Continuum Publishing Group Inc
370 Lexington Avenue, New York, NY 10017

The Continuum International Publishing Group Ltd
Wellington House, 125 Strand, London WC2R 0BB

Original German edition: *Die Zukunft des Universums:
Zufall, Chaos, Gott?* © 1997 Patmos Verlag Düsseldorf

English translation Copyright © 2000 by Arnold Benz

Printed in the United States of America

Library of Congress Cataloging-in-Publication Data
Benz, A. O.
    [Zukunft des Universums. English]
    The future of the universe : chance, chaos, God? / by Arnold Benz.
      p. cm.
    Includes bibliographical references (p.) and index.
    ISBN 0-8264-1220-3
    1. Religion and science.   I. Title.

BL240.2 .B44313   2000
291.1'75—dc21

                                              99-056794

For our children
Renate, Christoph,
Pascal, and Simon
at the beginning
of the new millennium

If we knew to perceive, who knows
whether truth would not, now and then,
actually appear in reality.

Kurt Marti, 1995

CONTENTS

INTRODUCTION

As a young physics student, I heard for the first time of theologian Karl Barth's postulate that science and faith had nothing, absolutely nothing, to do with each other. I cannot remember now just how I came upon this thesis; but I do remember, as though it were yesterday, the feeling it engendered in me. I suddenly felt liberated from the pressure that apparent proofs for the existence of God kept exerting on me. The usual arguments sponsored by "natural theology," which sought to draw conclusions about the character and existence of God from our knowledge of nature, I now began to find strained and insincere. For a theologian was now declaring God to be "wholly other," one who could never be known by derivation the way one derived the law of energy conservation from measurements and observations. This judgment corresponded exactly to my own sense of things as I confronted a daily flood of equations and experiments.

But what then is this God? Is God still conceivable at all in a modern or postmodern age largely shaped by science? These questions, which have preoccupied me ever since, eventually gave rise to this book.

To be sure, the divorce between theology and science is well accepted, at least from the theological side. Those great disputes associated with the names of Galileo and Darwin have died away in the lecture halls, and Galileo has been rehabilitated. Rules of polite distance now prevail.

Nonetheless, the word "God" shows up increasingly in popular works about modern physics. The concept appears there mostly in connection with unanswered questions about cosmology, life, human consciousness, or the character of reality—issues that currently represent the great enigmas of nature and define major goals of scientific research. Even though these questions are, in fact, obvious points of contact, they are apparently not the right places to initiate dialogue with theologians. The problem is that on the physics side the usually assumed concept of God[1] is borrowed from natural theology, from which contemporary theologians have long since distanced themselves. Here I do not assume God to be a mysterious key to further decipher scientific findings, as piously claimed by some scientists and vigorously rejected by others. I start from the premise that God is a concept originating from different perceptions and experiences. Contrary to the extreme views of the young Barth, this other reality cannot be detached completely from science.

Thus, from the side of theology, there should be growing interest in scientific matters, an interest stimulated at least partly by the realization that ethical and conceptual values must be communicated today in language colored by science. Then, too, the notion of seeking some universal if partly unknowable totality of reality is deeply rooted in religious tradition.

It is not the goal of this little book to outline a unified theory of faith and science. These two spheres of human experience, if one takes them seriously, resist seamless integration and complete harmonization. The borders between them remain defined even when one crosses from one to the other. The laws of each domain warrant respect. So isn't it foolish of me to adventure into foreign territory? Shouldn't scientists keep their possibly amateurish insights concerning culture and religion to themselves? I have had many such questions and doubts along the way. But I have finally moved beyond them for the sake of expanding my vision and fulfilling what I perceive to be a scientist's broader vocation in society. For within the past four hundred years, science has effected radical changes in human understanding and society; and it continues to do so. Scientists cannot remove themselves from responsibility in the midst of such change. I think they are obliged, on occasion, to expose their own personal, subjective responses to what they are discovering—provisional though these responses may be.

I find it telling that, following one of the many lectures on astronomy I give for a general audience, a young man remarked to me as we were leaving the room, "If the universe is as big as you have declared it to be, God must be even much bigger." Neither the subtle problems of how stars develop nor the unsolved riddles of how galaxies are formed had stirred his interest—but rather, a question of belief that my presentation had not addressed at all. When scientists present their knowledge on a rational level, lay people often feel themselves addressed on an existential level and enabled thereby to experience their "I" as part of the cosmos. Some go so far as to develop something of a personal relation to heavenly bodies. They not only want to hear explanations about the origins of natural phenomena but also to develop an emotional connection with the cosmos or, quite simply, the capacity to wonder at it all.

I proceed in this book from the assumption that faith and science are two different approaches to experiencing reality. With Karl Barth, I am still of the opinion that one cannot place professions of faith and scientific theories in direct connection to one another. It is not possible to proceed conclusively from one to the other; one side can neither prove nor disprove the other. Faith and science define two different planes that do not intersect. Both impinge on human experience, and neither can purport to offer the complete truth. But it is possible for an observer informed about both planes of inquiry to reflect on how they might relate. To achieve this, the observer must take an outside vantage point and view them within the metaspace of human perception and understanding. It is important to ponder the methodological foundations of both approaches. Actual mediation, however, is best pursued on a pragmatic level. For this reason, the practical and most relevant example, the future of the universe and ourselves as anticipated in faith and science, is a central theme of this book.

In this book, I try to take both realms—of faith and of science—fully in earnest. By *faith* I mean the individual and personal method of bringing God, the world, and individual human existence into relation with one another. I will make use of the religious system of Christianity, whose well developed theological concepts and traditions offer considerable insight into the existential issues I address. In the past, other religious systems have been considered in relation to physics and spirituality. By taking faith "in earnest" I mean that I do not rely solely on religious categories accidentally acquired in my youth, but draw on the latest forms of theological inquiry. My approach differs, then, from that of a good many physicists, who reduce religion to a low-grade metaphysics designed to answer questions for which science presumably knows no answer, or who end up showing that this metaphysical God is superfluous.

They still rely implicitly on an image of God left over from the age of Enlightenment, an image that is scarcely the only one available or the best informed by modern theology.

Science as such will also be taken seriously. Even though Karl Popper reminds us that all scientific knowledge and all theories are open to be proven false and may be encumbered by error, they nevertheless stand the test of pragmatic application when it comes to flying to the moon and returning again safely. Science does not renounce its own effectiveness; its occasionally dangerous applications in nuclear and gene technology may be recalled. Another unserious way of treating science would be to select only those scientific findings that are apparently compatible with preconceived opinions. The impulse to screen out undesirable evidence is by no means limited to religious fundamentalism.

In the pages that follow, I expound the thesis that it is senseless to seek God in the first moment of the Big Bang. Most of what matters for us and for the rest of the world originates afterwards and is not predetermined by conditions at the very beginning. Hence the futuristic emphasis of my title differs intentionally from the more familiar supposition that everything can be explained by recovering knowledge of some once-and-for all, pure moment of creation. I doubt also that God can be located directly in any of the boundary conditions, observations, and equations of science or within one of the remaining gaps in our knowledge. Even if God could be found there, I doubt whether a "God of the gaps" is worth pursuing, much less worshiping. Knowledge of God requires instead a quite different mode of perception from that used in scientific research.

As I was writing, I thought particularly of those readers who are fascinated by the overwhelming body of new scientific discoveries emerging in our day but who do not need to learn about the latest findings in great detail. I have tried not to presuppose specialized knowledge. When scientific terms are not explained more closely, the reader may presume that their technical import is not crucial in the current context or that more will be said about them in connection with a later topic. My envisaged reader is also interested in our inherited Western culture, particularly in its religious dimension. In view of the far-reaching changes affecting global culture, I see religious knowledge as requiring not just the preservation of venerable truths but also the discovery of new understanding. And at times I have written to myself and learned much from the process.

If some of this inspires others to reflect and discuss, the book will reach its goal.

Finally, though, the sort of understanding with which I am concerned here is not simply a theoretical knowledge without obligation. True religion touches one's innermost being, or else it remains a metaphysics of no consequence. I am cognizant that, with this very personal book, I am leaving the realm of "hard science" for the sake of inviting you, dear reader, to join me on this journey into a little explored, liminal territory that yet contains much of human interest. Mediating between these two planes of perception, given by science and religion, could be described as the greatest intellectual adventure of our time. This venture involves orienting ourselves in the modern world and discerning as best we can the meaning of the whole. It also involves the effort to cultivate intellectually the immense "new world" staked out by science so as to render it habitable for humans. The journey confronts us with decidedly disparate perceptions along the way, reminding us repeatedly of the great gulf between faith and science. Yet in the foreground stands the decisive and uniting question: What might we expect, and what might we hope for, from the future?

Part 1

UNIVERSE, TIME, AND CREATION

A NIGHT AT THE VERY LARGE ARRAY

Nothing is working any more, I have to go. We have tried all day to receive radio waves from the close binary star EM Cygni with the Very Large Array.[2] The source is weak, and I still don't know whether the interferometer has discovered the stellar system at all yet. In climatized rooms without windows somewhere in the state of New Mexico, we have entered millions of numbers, have checked, calibrated, added, transformed, saved them to tape, made mistakes, begun again, and still we have no image. LISTR, FILLM, UVLOD, UCAT, SETJY, MX—the computer programs make my head spin.

With the visitor's car I drive alone southwards, until no telescope, no power line tower can be seen, and get out. It is a clear, moonless night; I walk leisurely uphill.

As my eyes become accustomed to the darkness, I see the grandiose San Augustin plains with mountains on the horizon. Horizon? A splendid starry sky arches over it, as one can only experience in the desert and the mountains. No, my horizon is further off: Cygnus still shines in the west, the constellation of the Swan. Both of my stars must be somewhere therein, about a thousand light years distant and with a magnitude of 14.2—not visible to the naked eye. I can imagine them readily: the tiny, dazzling white dwarf, as large as the Earth, is surrounded by an accretion disk and reminds one of Saturn. The color of the disk is bright violet at the inner rim and changes outwards over blue and green to become red like a rainbow. Not far away, as far distant as the Moon is from the Earth and a thousand times larger, a reddish companion circles, somewhat deformed by the powerful attraction of the dwarf. Matter falls constantly from this body onto the disk, which in turn gives it up to the dwarf. Many other stars are in this region of the sky. The Swan lies in the Milky Way, glowing with stars. My scientific background makes it clear to me that the eye can only make out three thousand stars, but I can sense the billions of them.

I come to the summit, eager to see the other side and to witness perhaps a totally different view.

The center of the Milky Way lies somewhat under the Swan and has just set. The two hundred billion stars in our galaxy rotate around this center as on a carousel ride. I have the feeling that I am flying together with the solar system and the neighboring stars at the breakneck speed of over two hundred kilometers per second westward, directly toward this Swan.

It takes the Sun 240 million years to make a revolution in the Milky Way, a "galactic year." As it flew through its present position the last time around, the Permian Period was giving way to the Triassic on Earth. After an ice age and great flooding, the dinosaurs were just beginning to develop. The carousel begins to rotate. Decades fly with it, my lifetime and future centuries. The Milky Way will not change much until the turn of the next millennium. After a million years, the solar system will be located about where EM Cygni is at present. By then, the little white dwarf will have been so well fed by its companion that it will explode as a supernova. Obviously both of them will no longer be at the same location; they will have rotated along with the others. But a few million years later, our neighboring star Sirius will explode. There is movement on the carousel, as the passengers change or disappear, and new ones originate. Colorful clouds of gas appear and become star clusters. There is a huge coming and going. Through the development of stars, heavy chemical elements accumulate and the colors change. Even the Milky Way changes. Its spiral structure, with its two main arms, opens up. New spiral segments emerge and vanish. After many revolutions the galactic disk becomes flatter and contracts.

I feel as though I am sucked into the vortex, becoming a part of the mighty dynamic. My inner clock appears to run on another time scale, synchronized with the Milky Way. I am small compared with these stellar giants yet intellectually great, insofar as I am conscious of the spectacle. But size no longer matters since I am one with the universe. For a moment, I sense the limits of my personhood falling away; the intellect, which has spent all day in the same corner of my brain, seems to expand without limit. I am reconciled with nature and have no need to snatch any secrets away. The marveling "ah" is my speechless answer to this dialogue with the universe. For a moment there is no objective distancing and no obligation to explain that could separate me from the whole.

As I descend, I ask myself what was real about this experience. What do these feelings mean, this mystical fusion? Undoubtedly the experience had an effect, for I have changed, am content and newly motivated to carry on tomorrow with scientific work. No doubt, this psychological response was real and objectively perceivable also by others.

Was there more than stars, galaxies, and the universe? Had I perceived God? How does one identify a religious experience? Curiously enough, these questions first arise afterwards, upon reflection. At the time of the actual experience, they were not important.

THE TIME OF STARS

In the twentieth century, astronomy (*nomos* Greek = custom, order) has developed from a descriptive science into explanatory astrophysics. Today it seeks to understand the history of the cosmos. It concerns itself especially with these questions: How have the objects in the universe arisen, and how has the universe itself come to be? This chapter should show how astrophysics arrives at its explanations. An example involving stars will illustrate how the cosmos developed.

The opportunities for observation in astrophysics have multiplied in recent years. Radio waves and infrared radiation penetrate the interstellar gas from which stars form, and offer pictures of the birth of stars. Motions of stars and gas are measured today with an accuracy of a few meters per second. Space telescopes produce pictures that, until now, have never been so sharp, and they also capture ultraviolet light and X-rays from the universe. Intercontinental radio interferometry sees spatial details up to a thousandth of an arcsecond in sharpness. Observing from a distance of a hundred miles with this resolution, one could count the hairs on a human head or recognize astronauts on the moon.

Astrophysics has, in recent years, begun to understand how stars arise and perish. It recognizes that stars are not unchanging, eternal formations, but rather the luster of energetic processes on enormous scales of energy and time. The origin and life of stars is measured in millions and billions of years. A star draws its energy out of the fusion of hydrogen into helium and, in the later stages, into heavier elements. According to their size, stars give a considerable part of their mass back again to the interstellar gas in the Milky Way in the course of their development. Therefore a star is not a purely localized process. Stars alter our galaxy and, thereby, the surroundings of future generations of stars. Recent insight into the dynamics of the universe has made time an important factor in the physics of the heavens.

The formation time of stars exceeds human dimensions by far and compels astrophysics to draw the course of time from still pictures. Some stars group themselves into clusters containing hundreds to millions of stars that have arisen within a few million years—in astronomical terms, almost simultaneously. A star cluster, then, is comparable to a class of school children who are about the same age but differ in size and development. One observes in star clusters that more massive stars develop faster. Interestingly, the large stars beyond a certain mass, depending on the age of the cluster, are missing. What has become of them will be explained in the following.

A Star Is Formed

In our present-day Milky Way, about ten protostars per year begin to fuse hydrogen. The birth and prehistory of a star last approximately ten million years, so that roughly a hundred million stars are now being born in our astronomical neighborhood. Taken as a whole, the Milky Way today includes more than two hundred billion stars. There are hundreds of billions of such star collections, named "galaxies" after the Greek word *galaxis* for the Milky Way.

Stars originate in interstellar molecular clouds, which are well known for their beautiful, cloudlike dark structures. The gas of these nebulae is so thin that only a thousand atoms or less are contained in a cubic centimeter. Occasionally the density can also be a thousand times higher, but it is, even so, about a billion times lower than in terrestrial clouds. The density of interstellar gas is comparable to the thinnest vacuum produced in terrestrial laboratories. In places where the gas is denser than that which surrounds it, the gravitational force of the density fluctuation attracts the ambient gas. Thus, the concentration increases and incorporates even more gas. The process becomes self-enhancing. Smaller fluctuations are swallowed by larger ones or join together. The law of the fishes rules: the large eat the small. Mass concentrates slowly into a dense core (Fig. 1) until it collapses under its own gravity. Then the gas precip-

Figure 1: In molecular clouds with a diameter of a few hundred light years, here in the Eagle Nebula, dense cores form, out of which stars arise. Bright stars are already to be seen at upper right. They heat up the interstellar gas and blow it out of their vicinity. The cloud cores of dense gas oppose the pressure and protrude out of the present rim of the cloud (Photo: NASA).

itates toward the core's center in free fall. The initial movements in the collapsing gas are accidental and even themselves out largely, though not completely. A remnant of the momentum produces a gentle circular motion, which accelerates in the contraction process, something like the pirouette of an ice skating dancer. A vortex forms, rotating faster and faster the more it draws together. The angular momentum of the vortex forces the gas mass into the form of a rotating disk. These so-called accretion disks[3] are typical for newly formed heavenly bodies.

After ten million years the temperature and the density in the center is so great that the fusion of hydrogen into helium is set in motion and nuclear energy of stupendous proportions is unleashed. The additional gas pressure, which arises from the new source of energy, stops the contraction. In the innermost part of the vortex, an equilibrium is reached between gravity and gas pressure: the star is born.

Only infrared and radio waves can escape from inside the nebula and be observed. The dense gas surrounding the new star completely absorbs the optical light and is thereby heated up. This hot atmosphere of the young star impedes further growth and with it, the formation of an oversized massive star. For this reason, the mass of the largest of the known stars surpasses that of the smallest by a factor of only a thousand. A few million years must pass until the covering of excess gas is completely thrown off, like the cocoon of a caterpillar, so that the star becomes optically visible. Out of the ejected gas more stars arise—under certain circumstances, a whole star cluster.

Star formation is a good example of a *self-organizing process*, which begins without any direct outward influence and develops in chaotic fashion. The term "chaos,"[4] as explained in Part 4, means that one cannot predict the process over a long period of time at the level of particles and fluid elements. Star formation is impelled forward by its own gravitational energy and rids itself of heat in the form of radiation. Finally the contraction process stabilizes as a protostar. One could denote it as a saturation state for concentrations in interstellar molecular clouds. Such a stable solution of a system of equations, asymptotic after a long time, is termed an "attractor" in mathematics. This is the state of equilibrium toward which all star development aspires.

A star also develops further after it has formed. About a hundred light years distant, for example, lies EK Draconis, a younger sibling of the Sun. This star has the same mass and a similar inner structure, but is only seventy million years old. It differs substantially from the 4.6 billion year-old Sun through its far greater activity. Enormous eruptions shake it almost without pause, and a ten million degree hot corona, whose ultraviolet radiation is a hundred times stronger than that of the Sun surrounds it. Both the activity and corona originate from strong magnetic fields which arise from the short rotation of only 2.8 days. The generation and dissipation of magnetic fields constitutes an energy loss. It has slowed the Sun's rotation so that it turns at present a good ten times slower than the agitated EK Draconis. The Sun in earlier years must have had equally intense ultraviolet radiation, which may have been crucial for biological development on Earth to begin. The energetic emissions must have influenced considerably biological evolution also in later phases. Yet many of the higher forms of life, including the human being, could not withstand that early radiation dose. Fortunately, the Sun did not remain as it was but continued to develop. In the following subchapter and in a later chapter, we shall see how this development will proceed over a long period of time so as to render the Earth finally uninhabitable.

The Terminus of a Star

In another 4.8 billion years, the Sun will be comparable to the star Beta Hydri. Although Beta Hydri is only twenty light years distant, no indication of magnetic activity has been detected. The star has already used up about twenty percent of its hydrogen and is 1.6 times as large as the Sun. Because the combustion zone moved outward from its original place in the star's core, the structure of the star changed. The core became denser so that the star now produces more heat than the Sun. The star's surface has consequently expanded. As soon as an even greater portion of the hydrogen is used up, the star will become so large that the surface will cool down and become red. The aging star will become a red giant. The excess pressure that prevails in the atmosphere of red giants propels a strong stellar wind.[5] Sometimes the star loses whole layers of its atmosphere. These expand in the course of time and form spherical shells, which constitute so-called planetary nebulae with splendid colors. Nevertheless, these have nothing to do with planets. In the core, the helium cinders now become combustion material for a new nuclear fire, in which helium fuses into heavy elements such as carbon, nitrogen, and oxygen. After a few ten million years, red giants shrink into white dwarfs. The pictorial names should not lead to false assumptions that this involves a pretty world of fairy tale: the surface of a white dwarf is white because it is over ten thousand degrees hot. White dwarfs cool down slowly over many billions of years.

The development of stars that are more massive than the Sun proceeds more dramatically. Because the pressure generated by gravity is higher in the interior, the atomic nuclei fuse much faster and the development does not stop with oxygen. Heavier and heavier elements form— for example, silicon and magnesium. If the star has sufficient mass, nuclear synthesis engenders iron. In this stage of development, the star has an onion peel-like structure. Underneath the outermost hydrogen layer reside layers of helium, carbon, and silicon, wherever the corresponding nuclear reaction takes place. These processes do not yield much more energy, but they are significant for the chemical development of the universe. Old stars are like pressure cookers, in which the heavy elements are brewed. They are the sole origin of these important structural materials of planets and living creatures. In their later phase, massive stars unleash extremely strong stellar winds which are only a few thousand degrees warm and dense enough so that molecules and even dust particles form from carbon atoms and other heavy elements. Molecules and dust are swept along. In this manner, the stars often blow off more than half their mass into interstellar space. The greatest part of the carbon, nitrogen, and oxygen in the universe originates and is brought into circulation in this way.

After the massive star has also used up these new energy reserves of nucleosynthesis, it contracts further. The gravitational pull increases so much that the gas pressure can no longer compensate. The star then suddenly collapses in its interior. Still crumbling and under gigantic pressure, it makes its last source of energy accessible. Now nuclei with almost any size you choose can be built up. Most are unstable and disintegrate immediately, yet this implosion of a single moment produces all elements heavier than iron. All of the gold, lead, and uranium in the universe must have been formed in this manner.

This final discharge of nuclear energy happens in less than one second and pushes the gas pressure so high that the star explodes as a supernova. The larger part of its mass, a highly radioactive gas, is catapulted into space. In our Milky Way there occurs about one supernova per century. What is left is a neutron star, a kind of giant atomic nucleus, with approximately the Sun's mass yet with a diameter of only twenty kilometers. If it had more than two and a half times this mass, the nucleus would implode and form a black hole[6]—that is, a region of great gravitational pull out of which nothing, not even radiation, can escape any more. Neutron stars and black holes practically cease their development if no new matter is introduced.

New Generations of Stars

It may not be a surprise that stars are eventually extinguished and, as white dwarfs, neutron stars or black holes spirit their way invisibly throughout the Milky Way. In fact every splendor and each unleashing of energy must come to an end at some time. It is, however, exactly this late phase of the stars that is astonishingly creative. Stars are not simply snuffed out like a candle, but rather return a large part of their matter to interstellar gas. Significantly, this material is no longer the original, pure hydrogen with some helium from the primordial past of the universe, but a gas enriched with heavy elements. It includes grains of dust made up of ice, carbon, silicon, and iron. Stars are not born and then die in eternal circulation, but bring about a chemical change and the development of interstellar gases.

The lifetime among stars differs widely. A massive star fifty times the mass of the Sun remains only about a million years in such equilibrium that enables nuclear fusion to occur. Stars with the Sun's mass live ten billion years, and stars with less than 0.8 of the Sun's mass live longer than the present age of the universe. These small stars from all epochs of the Milky Way still exist and are observable today. They document galactic history.

In each new generation of stars, massive stars end as supernovae and increase the portion of heavy elements in interstellar gas, out of which new stars form again. The expelled materials from many stars are so mixed together that it would be difficult to reconstruct their original sources. A star of the younger generation contains contributions from many old stars. During this development, the smaller stars live on. Their chemical content is a fossillike inventory of the conditions of the gas at the time of their birth. Small, very old stars have been found with a thousand times smaller portion of metal than the still relatively youthful Sun contains. The products of fusion from the old, collapsed stars alter the development of the new generation of stars. They accelerate, for example, the nuclear fusion and shorten the lifetime of later generations of stars. Still more significant for us is the dust that is embedded in the gas. It shields the gas from the strong ultraviolet radiation of neighboring stars that would heat up the interstellar cloud. In these shaded, cool crannies, a number of smaller stars about the size of the Sun, but whose formation takes longer, can also originate.

Let us pursue the subject of this dust further (Fig. 2): As the stellar winds and supernova expulsions of extinguished stars encounter interstellar gas, the gas occasionally gets compressed. Such locations in turn serve as condensational seeds for new stars.[7] In the second or higher generations of stars, the dust follows the initial contraction and disk formation. If, however, the gas pressure and the radiation of the young star seek to

Figure 2: In the star cluster of the Pleiades, all of the stars are about 100 million years old. Most of the interstellar gas was blown away by young stars. Dusty remnants of the cloud out of which the stars originated are left behind as cirrus-like veils illuminated in the starlight (Photo: Mount Palomar).

push the superfluous material away, the sluggish dust grains remain behind and form a dust disk around the young star, as is often revealed by the infrared heat radiation of such structures. There are local concentrations also in dust disks that have arisen out of the density variations in the gas cloud and that have lost the race against the somewhat faster growing protostar. They swirl with the disk around the protostar and gradually incorporate many smaller and smallest agglomerations of dust, so that finally planets form. About a hundred million years pass until the dust particles end up in protoplanets or are catapulted outward through close encounters with planets. For another half billion years, the planets are still not in a restful state but intensively bombarded by small planets and interplanetary rubble.

After this stormy time, planets develop relatively little over billions of years, so that, under very special conditions, perhaps life can develop on them. However, dust, large pieces of rock as well as icy comets are still present today in the solar system. The debris from comet Shoemaker-Levy impacting on Jupiter in 1994 makes one realize that planet formation is not yet completely concluded. The Earth is targeted less often by comets and large meteorites because it is smaller and lies deeper inside the solar system than Jupiter. The last impact onto the Earth of a body as large as Shoemaker-Levy occurred 65 million years ago.

The Universe Develops

The origin of stars of higher generations and of planets shows how the old and bygone can become the jumping-off point for new development. In the realm of stars, time does not pass in cyclical fashion; each time the passage is a little different, and is never repeated exactly. For example, every new generation differentiates itself from the old in its chemical composition. The evidence for development is impressive. All the atoms that are heavier than lithium on our Earth bear witness to the history of the Milky Way. The carbon and oxygen in our bodies stem from the helium combustion zone of an old star. Two silicon nuclei, merged in the early phase of a supernova explosion, become the iron in our blood's hemoglobin. The calcium in our teeth formed during a supernova out of oxygen and silicon. The flouride with which we brush our teeth was produced in a rare neutrino interaction with neon. The iodine in our thyroid glands arose through neutron capture at the onset of a supernova. We are connected directly with the development of stars and are ourselves part of the cosmic history.

It would be incorrect to equate the origin of the cosmos with the Big Bang,[8] about fourteen billion years ago, just as it would be wrong to compare cosmic history to the running of a clock. A clock is made in a factory once and for all. Each piece of clockwork remains, one hopes, as it was made. Not so the universe: the prerequisites for forming most of the objects in the present universe have only appeared over the course of time.

✦ Galaxies and stars, for example, could originate, at the earliest a half million years after the Big Bang, when the temperature and the density of matter had become so small that the universe became transparent. Prior to this, radiation pressure prevented concentrations in the gas. Now matter uncoupled itself from the radiation, forming protostars which radiated the heat of their contraction irreversibly away. The fluctuations could increase.

✦ The first stars still had no planets composed of stone and iron. Planets like the Earth formed, at the earliest, with the second generation of stars.

The formation of the present universe has proceeded in an extraordinarily creative fashion; it has unlocked qualitatively new dimensions of development. Not only have new structures come about, but these have in turn created more novel possibilities for the unfolding of the universe. Creativity grew incrementally. With every step of development, a new category of objects originated. To be sure, their parts were in place at an earlier time, but the order and organization that came about formed a new unity.

In what direction does this development go? The extreme long-term processes are still too little known to make detailed predictions reaching beyond the Sun's lifetime and over hundreds of billions of years. Even those already known occurrences in the universe, above all the formation of stars and planets out of clouds of gas and dust, cannot simply be calculated in advance and recall the problem of predicting earthly weather. Undoubtedly, galactic dynamics is chaotic in the mathematical sense and therefore resists long-term prognoses. It is also certain that our Milky Way will not persist in its current condition, as we shall consider later. On this point, the future and the past are similar: both lose themselves in darkness.

When we look up at the starry sky on a clear night and believe that at least the stars are the same as always, this impression arises from the fact that our time-scale is too small. In reality, the universe has a stupendous dynamic; the origin of stars and formation of planets only represents a segment of processes that build upon earlier cosmic events such as the formation of matter out of quarks in the early universe and the origin of galaxies. Time plays a crucial role in the universe. Qualitative development is a fundamental characteristic of the cosmos.

CONFLICT OR DISTANCE?

Now I would propose setting the physical explanation of the world, as illustrated in the example of star formation in the last chapter, beside religious stories of creation. How compatible are modern science and the concept of creation? The answer has to do with the perception of reality. Mystical perceptions of wholeness and astrophysics are vivid examples of the variety and richness of our experience. The perception of time already depends on one's standpoint, whether we are participating in or only observing an event. Science and religion differ fundamentally not only in their points of departure but even more generally in their ways of perception and how to deal with the same.

Causality and Time in Science

Insofar as creativity in the universe was discussed in the last chapter, one might suppose that a creator must logically play a role in the drama. That is not so. In the course of the universe's development, the new did not arise out of nothing, but out of what was present, and in accord with causal laws. Although something new can perhaps appear in ways completely unforeseen—like a sudden change of weather—it is actually determined by what came before. With such unpredictable processes, one speaks of "deterministic chaos." Deterministic means that in principle the new is causally explainable, albeit only in retrospect. Science wants to explain objectively perceived phenomena. These explanations take on quite specific forms, according to the specialized area of study.

Since the seventeenth century, in particular with Galileo and Newton, increasing numbers of natural processes in the physical-chemical area can be described by differential equations. In order to remain generally understandable, this book will not contain any equations. This format should not lead to the impression that physics, chemistry, and other sciences could do without equations. On the contrary, and to the despair of many students, differential equations are actually the core of contemporary science. They yield the time change of a variable as a result of some cause and its duration. Time connects cause and effect. Without ongoing time, no causality is conceivable.

Interestingly enough, the basic equations of modern physics appear to be reversible with time. In the general theory of relativity, time appears as the fourth dimension and is to this extent not essentially different from space. That would mean that in principle cause and effect could be exchanged, something like the way a mirror reverses left and right. Supposing that a magician knows a trick by which time could be reversed, we would experience the world as if viewing a film run backwards. Clocks would show time to decrease. There are reversible processes as, for example, a swinging pendulum. One could run the film of a reversible process backwards without the viewer finding it unrealistic. With most films shown in movie theaters, it would soon be clear in which direction they are being shown. Obviously, human life is not reversible.

The concept of reversible processes, especially popular in the nineteenth century, is impressed with the paradigm of a mechanical universe that functions as predictably as a clock. One can easily imagine how the cog wheels of a clockwork can run in both directions. The roots of the concept of reversible time reach back into antiquity. In the Ptolemaic worldview, the unchanging heavenly bodies moved in circular orbits in perfect symmetry, in space as well as in time. If time were to run backwards, nothing would be altered except for the sense of revolution. The movement of heavenly spheres was no actual alteration. In the heavens, eternity reigned. A whiff of such timelessness can be detected in present-day discussions of the reversibility of time.[9] Today we know that the movement of a planet around the Sun is not completely reversible. Some minute radiation of gravitational waves is irreversibly lost, bringing the two heavenly bodies slowly but steadily closer.

In certain simple systems,[10] a time reversal would, in fact, alter practically nothing. That is especially so in the physics of elementary particles, where only a few objects are in the field of vision simultaneously. The processes of single elementary particles are symmetrical in future and past, and simulate a reversible time. The condition for a time-reversible system can be exactly stated.[11] In systems with many interacting parts, such as in reality is mostly the case, this condition is only rarely fulfilled and then only approximately. In the universe—as in life—we encounter a time that strides unmercifully forward. It is the asymmetry of time itself that enables us to speak at all about time in a flow of thoughts and words. In physics, the direction of time is often defined in relation to the second law of thermodynamics: a complex system develops into a state that is more probable than the initial condition. With this probability, the sense in which a film is running could be determined. The concept of "probability" already structures time in the factual past and possible future. This time structure precedes experience and must be generally valid. Irreversibility is therefore a necessary, a priori form in the ordering of scientific experience.[12]

Scientific explanations want to be causal and to tie observed natural processes with their origins. When the causes of natural events are known, they become predictable, capable of being manipulated, and technically applicable within a defined framework. Causality, however, is not endemic to all experience. In daily life, many familiar events occur without established causal relationship: we need only think of a spontaneous expression of the will. The pattern of cause and effect is much more a fundamental postulate of science; it defines and limits its domain of applicability.

At this point it is worth pointing out that the strict claim of causality in classic physics was relaxed in the 1920s through the quantum mechanics of Niels Bohr and Werner Heisenberg. According to this new physics of the microcosmos, position and momentum[13] of a particle at a given time are not exactly measurable. The product of inaccuracies in determining location and momentum is always greater than a specific value, the so-called Planck's constant.[14] It is everywhere and under all conditions equal. For an electron, for example, whose velocity is known with an accuracy of one tenth of a kilometer per hour, this means a blurred position of at least two millimeters. Since its initial condition is uncertain and not exactly given, some degree of chance is always connected with the result of a quantum process. Whether the electron passes through a one-millimeter opening in a screen cannot be calculated in advance. There is no causal basis that determines why one electron flies through the hole and another does not. The orbit of a particle is, however, not completely arbitrary; the possibility for chance is limited by Planck's constant. Through repeated experiments, the measured points of impact on a detector have a calculable mean value and adhere to a predetermined scattering law. In the sense that the probability, despite uncertainty, can be exactly calculated, quantum phenomena themselves are causal and deterministic.

That is why science cannot evidence God. According to its methods, it must presuppose causal origins and pursue its investigation as though there were no God.[15] The laws of cause and effect are a part of the method and never questioned. If no causal connection is found, this gap would not in itself prove the existence of God. Such a case has actually entered the picture, with the uncertainty of quantum physics. It was embodied in physics as a chance process for which there is no explanation. Even if a phenomenon resists any causal explanation, it would be difficult to prove it will do so forever. Science cannot depart from the field delimited by causality.

Religious Perception

By contrast, the apprehension noted in the first chapter is a perception of wholeness, as many people have experienced in similar fashion. The border between subject and object is momentarily lifted, and the perception transcends the person. In the following section I shall refer to it as a spontaneous *mystical perception*, without assuming the methods or the dogmatic structure of any particular mystic. I count these among general religious perceptions, which also include other manifestations.[16] In philosophy and theology today, one terms such occurrences "transcendental experiences" in the broadest sense, without identifying them necessarily with apprehensions of God. The episode recounted in the first chapter demonstrates better than any discursive definition could what I mean by this kind of perception.

Perceptions of wholeness are sensations of reality for those who experience them. This "knowledge" consists of impressive images. It cannot adequately be expressed by concepts that would satisfy science. What is perceived, in close relationship to the world or to God, can only be communicated in figurative terms; often much or most of such an experience remains unexpressed. Struggling to find the right words, one who relates the perception sometimes sounds odd as though lacking common sense. Questioned by reason, the report may appear absurd, not understandable, and like a stuttering of undefined words. It may not appeal to the listeners, even to those who have had similar personal experiences. When, however, it does resonate, it can also have great significance in the life of the listener or reader. Logical systems, entire world models and methods have been developed from reflection on mystical perceptions aimed at seeking to achieve again an altered state of consciousness or to attain a personal union with God.

The focus here is on the different modes of perceiving in science and in the mystical way. Perceptions of wholeness proceed through a state of consciousness in which feelings play an important role. A person feels unity, oneness with the whole, and participation in the world process. The spectrum of experiences is very broad. The ego can expand into the immeasurable; in other cases, the sense of human identity is completely lost. In a mystical perception, one views the world from another perspective; the body's spatial orientation can be lost for a certain period of time. The Greeks named this condition *ek-stasis* (placed outside of oneself). Particularly striking is the experience of time in mystical perception. Time either passes extremely fast or else it is perceived as standing still or absent. In mystical perception, time does not move synchronically with the wristwatch.

Reported perceptions of wholeness contain no scientific information about the universe. They can, however, leave important traces. If "reality" denotes what has a lasting effect in real life, these traces testify to the experienced reality. Surely, authenticity cannot be proven beyond doubt, and there are also mystical perceptions that appear to us as being apart from any reality. What the experience brings about objectively and noticeably to others might nevertheless be an indication of the reality of inner perception. Mystical perceptions are experienced above all by solitary individuals, which is why they often pass little noticed. Decisive events of the Judeo-Christian religious history have a mystical character—for example, the burning bush of Moses, or the transfiguration of Jesus. They are ground-breaking experiences at crucial turning points. I know of no religion that does not contain the mystical element of baring oneself and surrendering oneself to the whole.

At this juncture, a completely different kind of religious perception that plays a central role in Christianity and Judaism must also be remembered. It is the experience of the divine through faith. By "faith" I mean here a preunderstanding of reality. It is a knowledge that is necessary in order to perceive a certain dimension of reality.[17] This preunderstanding is based on trust and must be confirmed and strengthened through daily experiences. In existential crises, it is also put to crucial tests. Faith functions somewhat like a sensor for godly experiences in daily life.

I proceed from the important assumption that there can be no religious perception without a participating subject. God cannot be experienced, be it in mystical experiences or in daily trust, without a close connection between a person, the world, and God. The question then plausibly arises as to whether this reality can also exist without a subject. Would it exist in a universe without human beings? As a consequence of the above, this point cannot be established without participation. In the following, it is implicitly presupposed. I maintain firmly that religious perceptions are universally human, repeat themselves, and are communicable through metaphoric images.

Regarding reality, religious perceptions are similar to perceptions of art. The subject participates and is part of the perception process. Nevertheless, the experienced reality is not purely subjective as many, but not all, people are susceptible in a similar way to the same piece of art. In an artistic "revelation," the subject and the object are not separated in the Cartesian manner, assumed in scientific investigations. Such perceptions, disallowing any separation of object and subject, will be referred to as *participating perceptions*. They are at the basis of any religion.

The Function of Creation Stories

Not only modern science but also religions describe what constitutes the world and how it came into being. In order to take these narratives seriously in conjunction with our scientific worldview, we must, to begin with, take heed of their very different message. In biblical and in other stories of creation, it is vividly related that, at the beginning of the world, God or the gods created nature, from the creation of light to that of human beings. Even when the raw material of the creative act is mentioned, be it chaos, clay, or nothingness, little is said about the actual process of creation. Particularly consequential is the first story of creation in the Bible (Genesis 1), which refuses to describe the details of creation or to embellish it with speculation and fantasy. As in all other stories of creation, the "how" is unimportant compared to the question of "why," concerning order and substance in the cosmos. God is portrayed as Might, whose free will has caused nature to be created at divine discretion. God appears like an artist, whose creative technique matters less to the art lover than how the work appeals and what it personally signifies. An art historian may inquire about the technique of production, how the artist has mixed the colors and held the brush. To experience art, such how-questions are not essential. Stories of creation are likewise not theories in competition with scientific theories. The two operate on entirely different planes.

The differing goals and terms of scientific and religious accounts of formation can hardly be overlooked. Of course, one could read creation stories in a scientific manner, as if they were reports of an objective occurrence that an unrelated observer retells to another individual. Such a manner of reading has, in the past, already led to many misunderstandings and has still not been completely surmounted. Creation stories reflect the knowledge of their time, to be sure, but contain no additional *scientific* information. They do not describe the cause of a natural event or disclose how its genesis could be repeated in a laboratory. Not even a new measurement is proposed that could confirm any theory. No scientific journal would consent to publish such a report. The reduction of a creation story to its supposed scientific content would establish only that things are as they are because God made them so. Perhaps this is an answer one would, in exasperation, give a child who kept asking questions, but it is no scientific knowledge.

Creation stories are not scientific or journalistic writing of a neutral party, but communications about our personal significance, our task in life and responsibility in this world. They are less concerned with natural processes than with the meaning of things, their relationship to each other and to us. Neither are creation stories "infotainment." They do not seek simply to communicate objective facts, as in television reports, that one can take in while drinking a beer and then forget again. Unless people are willing to be moved, changed, and participate personally, creation stories make no sense.

Creation stories tell of a plan or a goal by which the creator acted. The essential point of interest is not the act itself but God's reasons. They are narrated in the form of pictorial and figurative story, which then establishes the reason why God, acting voluntarily, made things in such a way and what their actual character is. The stories of divine action relate the physical order with the ethical rules of the world and bestow models for human interaction. Creation stories seek to show the place of human beings in God's world and their task therein—that is, they mediate ethical values. This is their deepest meaning.

It must absolutely be kept in mind, at this point, that "acting" is a concept that stems from human experience and is attributed in a *metaphoric* sense to God. It is also important to understand that, without this figurative language, one cannot talk about creation. This form of speech will later be examined more closely. The metaphoric image of "acting" means, first and foremost, that the creator comes into direct contact with the world. Again, there is less interest in how this took place than in the intention. The characteristics of this acting (benevolent, responsible, and the like) are important and vary significantly in the different narratives.

What all creation stories have in common is the creator's faculty of free choice. What is this creative freedom? Freedom should not be confused with arbitrariness. It is not marked by vacillating decision-making: today this, tomorrow that. As the term originates from human experience and is again a metaphor, let us first consider freedom for decisions among humans. A person who is really free chooses his or her own way of life. In a given situation, he or she then acts accordingly, even though it were possible to do otherwise. Nevertheless, the ground for this acting is not a causally determined reason; unless it were an action performed out of pathological compulsions, and thus not free. The reasons for activity involving free will originate from a value system, and freedom consists in the choice of these values.[18] Consequently, God's "acting" may not manifest itself in erratic, unnatural interventions that go against the rules of God's creation.

Today one again often hears the word "creation" because, contrary to the more neutral "nature," it also implies values. A theology of creation is expected to provide orientation concerning the apparently limitless technical applications of science and should set limits as to how far human society can take control of nature for its own use. Such values are implied by the order inherent in a creation story. Thus, in the first biblical creation narrative, it is not difficult to find the specification of order and relations, from light and inanimate material up to human beings; with equal placement of man and woman, by the way. Nature, as known to science, does not become "creation" by simply adding a creator to it. A prerequisite to qualify the world as a creation is a view in which the relationship of humanity to nature, the individual's assignments and goals, as well as the essence and meaning of the universe are established.

The creation process is, even today, often still identified with the beginning of time or the start of the universe, corresponding to the paradigm of the clockwork-universe from deism in the eighteenth century. In the worldview of modern science, however, most of the things in the universe—from the stars to living creatures—find their origins over the course of time. In view of the development of the universe, it would make little sense to limit creation to the time of the Big Bang and to fix God's activity to this far-off point in time. Events in the early universe are, moreover, still scientifically controversial, the further back the more so, and therefore less appropriate as material for modern creation stories. To be meaningful again today and to permit the communication of values, creation must be brought into relationship with the scientifically acknowledged development of the universe from the Big Bang until today. The term *creatio continua* is employed in theology to mean the ongoing creative work of God, God's activity in time.

If belief in creation and science have different outcomes and answer different questions, one might conclude that all conflict and tension between them are misunderstandings and easy to remedy. This is not so! Though science is still far from understanding all the processes in the universe, there is at present no natural event that lies unequivocally outside its capacity to address. The very universe may have formed out of a vacuum, according to currently known natural laws. The remaining gaps are the province of present-day scientists, whose greatest goal is to shrink those gaps, even to close them. Because it is usual, with every gap that is bridged, for more gaps to emerge, scientists will not run out of work even in the long term. Nevertheless, there appears to be no basic gap in the development of the universe, from the Big Bang to the appearance of humankind, that could only be explained through the working of a supernatural power.

God's apparent absence from scientifically accessible reality is the basis for contemporary agnosticism. God can no longer be localized in the view of science, for, in the twentieth century, the cosmos became a part of the human realm of experience and is explainable according to physical laws that also hold on Earth. Acts of creation are scientifically unprovable despite all good intentions, and even though it is maintained otherwise among certain creationist circles. The creator has left no fingerprints behind. The conflict between science and creation belief seems unavoidable. In the following chapter, we consider whether and how one can discuss creation at all, in the present time, and under these conditions.

LET'S SEPARATE WHAT
DOES NOT BELONG TOGETHER!

Thus far we have considered the disparate purposes and functions of scientific and religious narratives. One could now go and select the story form according to the question posed: What is the causal origin? What does it mean to me? As a result, an intellectual uneasiness could well overtake one in view of the following questions:

+ Can a cosmic process—for example, the formation of a star—then be a causal phenomenon of nature, as well as a creative act on God's part?
+ How compatible is the determinism of natural processes with creative freedom?

This and the following chapter show that the opposing concepts—causality and creation, determinism and freedom—need not be regarded as mutually exclusive. In the first argument, not only the functions of both kinds of narratives but also both modes of perception and language will be sharply separated, so that a conflict becomes impossible. In a second argument, introduced in the next chapter and developed later, correspondences between scientific and religious perceptions are discussed so as to reveal how both ways of knowing share a common field of vision.

Two Levels of Perception

Causality and creation are terms drawn from different realms of perception and language that, in principle, do not relate to one another. They correspond to two distinctive methods of dealing with reality. In modern *science*, the object is examined through a directed manipulation or observation of causal connections. A subject experiments, poses questions, measures, and observes. The subject itself is not part of the experiment; it should have as little influence as possible on the result of the examination, and should be exchangeable. Subject and object remain separate, as much as possible. The result of these efforts is a *knowledge to dispose*, which, for example, clarifies a process so well that it becomes technically applicable.

In a creation story, on the other hand, the questioner does not deal directly with the object but listens to the reasons of its creator. The subject should not be indifferent to these but must draw the consequences in real life. The subjects are themselves created and, unlike the creator, find their places as creatures among their own. Persons who commit and entrust themselves to such a relation are therefore connected in a triangular relationship—subject, object, God—and are part of a greater whole including ultimately all creation. Creation has to do with this large web of meaning. This *knowledge of orientation* allows subjects to place themselves rightly in the world and to act meaningfully.

In this model of strictly separated levels of perception and language, discussions about truth find themselves only within their respective disciplines. Causal explanations are models of reality that can only be confirmed or disputed through new observations and experiments within science. No religious court of appeals can contradict a scientific theory *ex cathedra*.

On the other hand, the truth of a creation story only reveals itself in the life of a human being who believes—that is, who engages and trusts in the pertinent relation. Religious truth reveals itself in the character of a person's behavior. If the creation story emphasizes the commonness of all creation, it should, for example, prove to be life-promoting in practice. If then both levels of perception are methodically separated, a creation story does not address questions of truth in the scientific realm of reality.

Perception, Experience, Faith:
What Is Truth?

The sciences perceive reality with measurements and observations. These perceptions alone, however, do not explain reality, for the facts generally admit several explanations. A certain latitude is open to theoreticians seeking to develop a theory. In a theory, the observed facts are brought into coincidence with mental images. These images contain our thought structures, such as logic, concepts, mathematical models, and—in a preliminary or bad case—also our prejudices. A good theory can explain many observations and predict future occurences exactly. No scientific theory, however, can lay claim to being the sole truth. It is imaginable that a future test, using further measurements, could turn out to be negative. Thus there are no true and false theories, only theories that explain the available observations or contradict them. In this manner, sciences approach the truth ever more closely but can never state the absolute truth about an object.

Similarly, the truth of a creation story cannot be vindicated by the mystical or religious *perception* that perhaps lies behind the narrative. In a mystical experience, persons are physically informed of the environment through their bodily senses, but perceive reality directly in their innermost being and without the usual rational filter. The mystical "observer" passes through a close relationship or perceives a melting together of the outer and inner worlds. As with every perception, a mystic becomes aware of an outer object or an inner occurrence, and comprehends it only subjectively at first. The question of truth does not yet arise in the initial process, because nothing is consciously interpreted, it is only perceived.

In the connection between subjective perception and its object, an *experience* is built that may be confirmed in further perceptions and can be communicated to other people. These experiences are ordered and impressed with our patterns of thinking and our cultural background, in the case of religious as well as scientific experiences. Therefore, they do not communicate a wholly objective truth either in the view of modern science or of Plato. It is thus concluded here, in agreement with most of today's philosophers, that the actual truth does not derive from experience. But then what is truth?

For Plato, the *truth* consisted of ideas, unchanging archetypal pictures or concepts, which stand behind the appearance and are eternal. To recognize these truths—that is, to become aware of an idea—is what Plato terms *anamnesis* (Greek = remembrance, memory). For him, ideas possess a divine nature and can only be perceived by us if our senses also possess the divine receptor organ of anamnesis. With the Neo-Platonists and in ancient Christian philosophy, the Platonic ideas became the concepts of creation, or in the words of modern naturalists "God's plan." What, in the following, I speak of as *revelation* has much in common with anamnesis.

The biblical creation stories are no eyewitness reports, but rather are concerned with revelation. I do not understand why people have misconstrued the concept of revelation for so long—it is still so with a few—to mean that individual words fall from heaven. Only the actual content, the *essence* of the creation story, can be revealed. It effects a new view of reality, or rather, a new relationship to the world. The fact that at the beginning of the Bible two different creation narratives are set down proves that for the editors of Genesis individual words and elements of plot were not important in and of themselves. Moreover, there are further creation stories in the New Testament, in particular the prologue to the Gospel according to John. In Christianity, the story of Jesus and his resurrection becomes the central revelation and its major creation story.

How does a revelation come about? The writing down of words is only the last act. What comes before is most significant: the appropriation and acceptance of the actual content, an "aha!"-experience, or a startling awareness and awed reaction of the receiver of such a revelation. What can be stored and reproduced through data processing does not render it. Revelation only happens when listeners or readers are spoken to through the content. Revelation is, therefore, no neutral scientific information, whose essence consists of numbers and equations. It is not derived from natural or historical facts. It should also be noted that revelation is not coercive; one does not have to concern oneself with it, rather it is sensed as a gift.[19]

It is generally acknowledged that creation has to do with belief based on *faith*. Faith is a religion-based expectation that must be tested in daily life. In colloquial speech, belief and faith are often equated with deficient knowledge. That is not meant here. Instead "faith" means to rely completely on what one has recognized. To believe a creation story means to appropriate its values for oneself. To open oneself up to such a revelation is a risk and requires trust in advance, for its truth cannot be scrutinized at the moment. It is only when the effects this faith has on one's life are felt that the rightness of revelation may or may not be realized. The proof for a creation story is traceable a posteriori in life. Such evidence is connected to the subject and not capable of being objective; thus, it is not a scientific criterion of truth.

The methods of objective science and a faith capable of establishing relations could not be more different. Their perceptions, experience, and language operate on completely different levels. Even the easy metaphor of the "one reality regarded from two different angles" is faulty, in that it already objectifies reality. It pictures reality as a table standing between equal observers, who see it from different perspectives. This picture takes as a given the separation of object and subject. In the religious way of perception, however, a person is inextricably bound to reality and cannot be fully disengaged from it. That means, in relation to the metaphor of the table, that there is only one observer at a distance; the other is fused with the table. An unhappy image! Given these differing ways of perception, one cannot speak lightly of a single reality.

Consequences and Problems
of the Separation of Faith and Science

Both faith and science can only be taken in earnest when the differences between their ways of perception, their methods and goals, are recognized. Only with the separation of both domains, as Karl Barth promoted uncompromisingly over a half century ago, do they take on clear contours, with their potential and their limits readily visible.[20]

The separation between the level of the objective and the participatory level corresponds well to the Judeo-Christian idea of God's transcendence. The transcendental God is outside nature and in no scientifically comprehensible process is God directly discernible, not even in the formation of the universe. God's absence from natural processes should not be a surprise: indeed, it must be so if God and nature are distinguishable. God's lack of a discrete dwelling place in the modern universe should not be astonishing: one was simply not made aware of it as long as there was apparently ample space in heaven.

The separation in levels of perception and language permits the same universe, which science explains as causal, to be perceived also as creation. God is then involved in all, not only at the beginning but also in the new, in the scientifically understandable, as well as in the still unexplained. Notwithstanding, God does not proceed into causal processes in nature and is not to be associated with any natural event. God is transcendent in all.

The belief in creation therefore falls outside scientific criticism. Its criteria are exclusively religious perceptions, existential experiences, and the actuality of the world—its objects, processes, and laws. The divine "action" occurs on a plane to which science has no access and where acting is meant in a figurative sense. A causal explanation of, for example, the origin of stars, of life, or of humans, corresponds on the participatory level to a free and voluntary divine will. From the standpoint of science, conditioned by success, one could object that the methods of faith neither make Mars flights possible nor do they illuminate the secrets of the Big Bang. Yet true faith promises to give meaning and orientation to life as well as death, to bring balance and peace to humanity, and to the whole of creation.

Is this harmony through complete separation, however, not a lazy compromise? When the sciences and faith are divided, there is also no common language and thus no way of making faith understandable within the worldview of modern science. There could, for example, be no creation story written out of elements of scientific research, for the acts of creation would have no relation to natural events. Religious language would itself have to renounce metaphorical images from nature.

Common sense rebels against this; one wants to know how God acts in the world or else strike the word "God" from our vocabulary. If God cannot be traced in nature, how then should God exist?[21] The perception and linguistic idiom of the sciences increasingly supplants that of religion today. Fewer and fewer people still understand religious language. With a complete separation of faith and science, no clue would remain of how God acts in the world. There would be no interest in correspondences or parables. A sentence like "God made . . . the stars" and "set them in the dome of the sky to give light upon the earth" (Genesis 1:16–17 NRSV) would then stand totally ineffectual and without any relation to astrophysical statements about star formation. And can an ethic based on religion be understandable to scientific reason if God's acting remains incomprehensible? Is it sufficient to affirm that God has created the world, without involving the how-question? One remembers, for example, the difficult questions in the field of gene technology. When it concerns concrete ethical questions, both languages must, of necessity, encounter one another. One cannot remain solely with the Barthian separation of faith and science.

In the past few years, there have, therefore, been attempts by theologians to bring God's voluntary acting and the scientific understanding of nature into a mutual relationship.[22] A superior standpoint is necessary, from which faith and science can be viewed in a common perspective. Points of comparison and of nexus can then be determined, from which a discussion could sensibly begin.

NECESSARY RAPPROCHEMENT

The Nexus of Amazement

A possible point of encounter between faith and science could be sheer amazement. As an astronomer, I am often asked whether I can still stand in wonder at the immense size of the universe, the unimaginable time spans and the enormous energies unleashed. Amazement as a state of the subject's consciousness is set aside as contrary to the scientific method. And yet Aristotle, for example, sees just this amazement as the starting point for all science: proceeding from wonder over daily things, the human mind poses questions about ever-greater connections up to the origin of the universe.[23]

A child wonders about each new object. This amazement releases positive feelings, excites the joy of discovery, and stimulates learning. Adults also like to wonder at strange worlds and exotic customs. To well-tried researchers, amazement is not foreign. One may imagine Galileo's first look through the telescope at Jupiter's moons or Darwin's observations of finches on the Galapagos Islands. I must confess that I have largely grown accustomed to astronomical orders of magnitude. Like any amazement at something new, even these overwhelming numbers pale in time. The new and the great sooner or later become a part of our experienced world. We adjust our view of the world and our horizon accordingly.

Yet there remains a special kind of amazement: the awe-filled "ah, that's the way it is," over a surprising connection between bits of information that had seemed to be far apart or the simple beauty of an equation. Further intellectual effort and rational investigation cause it to lose nothing of its esthetic marvel. Again and again one encounters this meaningful relation, and every time one is amazed. It is not bewilderment at seeing a miracle, but the clarity after the fog of unknowing lifts that evokes this sense of wonder. In the following, I shall describe three observations that continuously provoke in me this reflective amazement.[24]

1. There is no indication that the order of nature, its fundamental laws and physical symmetries, have altered since the Big Bang. Laws of conservation and other basic equations were perhaps already valid at the beginning of the universe. It is amazing that, given the exactness of measurement, neither the mass of the electron nor the gravitational constant nor any other substantive constant has changed. Total energy, electrical charge, the number of leptons, and other fundamental parameters in the universe appear to have remained constant for over fourteen billion years.

2. I am amazed that, despite this constancy, even stubbornness, new objects have arisen in the course of the universe's development. This was only possible because the development itself developed. New dimensions of development opened up, for example, as galaxies and stars came to be, from which planets formed, and living creatures—as well as the human intellect—made their entrance. Imagine that we could place ourselves back into the early universe for a moment, a few seconds after the beginning: we are surrounded by a hot gas composed of only a few kinds of elementary particles. There are neither planets nor stars. The universe consists solely of a gas that is more evenly dispersed in all directions than terrestrial air, without clouds and without differences in altitude. We can hardly imagine that, out of this flat homogeneity, something so complex as living creatures would originate. The formation of the first structures, the clusters of galaxies and protogalaxies, were surprise enough. (This formation, incidentally, is not yet understood even today.) The further development from stars to planets up to a human creature would have been impossible for us to predict. From this viewpoint, the new came as absolutely unexpected, even though it might be causally explained later on.

3. The most elementary and, at the same time, most puzzling phenomenon in the universe is certainly time itself. Human ingenuity cannot seize and use time at its own disposal as it might in the case of space.

Time is also a basic condition of the development of the universe. Each small step in causality or in a chance process is not possible without a before and after, without a certain quantum in time. Whence does time come, and how do these ongoing new possibilities of development come about?

✦ ✦ ✦

These three sources of amazement form a remarkable unity. They depend on each other and form a close relationship. If the physical constants had not been so firmly preserved, life on Earth, for example, could not have formed. Without order nothing new can originate. Yet time, as a condition for development, appears to be more than a mere pattern of order in the universe. In combination with causal laws and with chance, it appears to have creative potential.

I find especially impressive and harmonious the fact that the whole of physics is grounded upon a few laws that can be mathematically formulated. Millions of observations of the atomic and subatomic world were successfully described in the last fifty years using a single theory, that of quantum mechanics. Its essence is Schrödinger's equation, according to which all of these natural processes function. The basic processes in nature appear to be simple. But the events on the next highest level, within the molecule, are already so intricate that they can only be approximately and with great effort traced back to the basic physical laws. As a result, chemistry requires new terms and concepts that are not found in the language of physics. Apparently the simple basic laws of the universe also include the possibility of highly complex connections toward a qualitative development. The more of this we understand, the more amazing the elegance and purposefulness of nature appears.

With this amazement, I move away from scientific objectivity. I enter into a relationship with the objects, permitting them to move out of the passive role and allowing them to have an effect on me.

The Crisis of Metaphysics

What in amazement goes beyond any doubt, upon reflection nonetheless presents a problem for comprehension. Who has not felt, in an emotionally buoyant mood while enjoying nature that, beyond the scientifically known facts, nature becomes transparent to reveal a mystery that signifies its true being? Philosophical metaphysics, which, in light of this feeling, sought to discuss the "thing-in-itself" or God, had already been questioned by Immanuel Kant and then, in the course of the nineteenth century, basically failed. At that time, the metaphysical theories of nature and notions of God expanded into a superstructure, built on experiences of nature. Adverse criticism had it that these speculations did not necessarily follow from scientific perceptions and that the conclusions were not convincing. The metaphysics of German idealism fell under the suspicion that it was ideological, that it expounded and defended a certain religious worldview.

A similar situation occurred with natural theology, from medieval scholasticism to the liberal theology of the nineteenth century, which attempted to chart a progression from natural phenomena to God. So, for example, the property of nature to be well disposed to humans in general was linked to the existence of a gracious creator. Through this linkage, God edged closer to the realm of science and became there an object of philosophical assertions and controversies. The attempt to extrapolate from nature to God had to fail because God and scientific reality lie on different levels. Similarly, what today causes one to wonder cannot be a scientifically compelling indication of God's direct action.

With the preconceived existential attitude of faith, however, the sense of wonder becomes a possible point of contact with science. From the standpoint of faith, scientific findings about the events and characteristics of the universe receive a hermeneutic function: they enable people to better comprehend what they already believe. Order, creativity, and time are points of conjunction to which faith as well as science have access. Scientific knowledge may thus bring forth indications and images that illustrate how one can understand the concept of creation in the modern worldview. It does not offer proof for faith in God but can relate faith to objective reality and make faith understandable for believers as well as nonbelievers.

Conversely, faith can also interpret the modern worldview. From the standpoint of faith, a "deeper dimension" in the universe is perceived through amazement. It is no direct recognition of God, but points nevertheless to the transcendental embedding of the cosmos in something comprehensive. To be sure, faith and science remain on different levels and cannot replace, but influence, each other. Only if both of them are already present can faith and science approach and help to interpret one another. With regard to the human search for meaning, as well as to an ethic of human pursuits relating to nature and especially in science, this type of close communication is necessary.

The Biblical Model

An example of how faith interprets a worldview can readily be found in the Old Testament creation stories. The theological vision based on faith and religious experience must clearly be distinguished from the world model that was shared by a much larger population than the people of Israel. The worldview of Genesis 1 originates, in fact, from the foreign Babylonian culture. It was used as a medium to express faith and ethical values in the frame of the concepts understandable at the time and to transmit a theological message.

According to the usual world model of antiquity, the Earth was conceived to be a disk, vaulted by a bell-shaped heaven. The materials of the creation stories—light, the great water over the firmament and underneath the disk of Earth, the sea dragons, the heavenly bodies, and so forth—were all general knowledge at that time in the Middle East. These elements are neither completely listed in lexicon-fashion nor explained, but they do provide the background for theological statements. It is exactly that knowledge of the world which enables discourse about creation to take place.

The antique situation differs from ours in a fundamental way. Genesis 1 is directed to an audience surrounded by a cultural milleu in which the objects of nature still extensively represented divine beings, believed to stand in close relation to humanity. Light, water, and heavenly bodies were not natural things as we understand them today. Rather, they incorporated threatening or helpful goddesses and gods or their realms. The biblical creation story unraveled this concept of the gods in nature, proclaiming the supposed gods as created things. The fabric of relationships remained so dense, however, that the audience did not feel like subjects separated from God and nature. The transcendence of God, as it was proclaimed in the narratives opposing the idea of gods in nature, requires no other language level, but rather a new valuation of the world and of the relationship of the subject to the world.

The biblical psalms are also expressions of faith and originate from a similar mental outlook. From the view of the world at that time, praise, gratitude, and petitions are brought before God. General knowledge, personal experience, and the revelations of the Old Testament are effortlessly bound together. The perspective is directed toward an acting creator, without casting a glance at questions such as how to explain the objects of praise, or how the petition should then be realized in actuality. God's action is like a mountain on the horizon, which marks the goal, not the way.

THE UNIVERSE AS A CREATION

I n this final chapter of the first part, I shall try to represent the scientifically explainable world in the expressive idiom of creation, analogous to the way it was done almost three thousand years ago. Dry words
and gray theory are less appropriate than an example. As a psalm is not so
directly reflective of mythical tradition, it may be more easily appreciated
in modern form than a creation story. I have appropriated the structure
and disposition of Psalm 19, a genuine psalm of creation. As far as it was
accessible to me, I have taken into consideration the modern results of
Old Testament research and have written a new version of the psalm re-
flecting the modern worldview on the foundation of New Testament tradition. In the psalms, the sense of wonder can already be found in the
psalmist's apprehension of the universe as well ordered and yet creative.

The sensation of wonder is today a significant nexus between faith and
science. It belongs to the basic pattern of a psalm to express relationship
among a human being, nature, and God. The metaphysics—one spoke of
"wisdom" at that time—is not without reference to the personal life of
the psalmist. The relationship of the person to God is embodied in praise
and prayer.

It is helpful to read the original of Psalm 19 along with the new version, since the former should in no way be replaced. For the inexperi-
enced Bible reader, it should be noted that psalms of creation are not to
be read as condensations in the popular science vein, but rather "with the
heart" like a poem.

A New Song of Praise

The cosmos glorifies God's greatness,
and all creatures praise the Master.
From galaxy to galaxy, knowledge spreads out,
one generation murmurs it to the next
with inaudible speech, a message without bytes.

From the edge of the universe,
10^{23} *kilometers distant,*
the light of quasars takes ten billion years
to reach our telescopes.
A hundred billion galaxies glide away
in expanding space
and another hundred billion stars
turn like a potter's wheel
around the mysterious kernel of each galaxy.
The radiance of the Sun,
surrendering each second a million times
the yearly energy consumption of humanity,
and the fullness of Earth have
brought forth a million kind of living creatures,
each in itself a wonder
of aptness and beauty.
High-molecular processes in cells
make life possible.
They are driven by millions of genes,
Works of art from thousands of nucleotides,
and each of these again a double ring of a dozen atoms,
nuclei encircled by an electron cloud,
in relation to Earth, so small,
as the Earth is in relation to the whole universe.

They all proclaim God's wisdom.
Gaps in knowledge are foreign to their language,
which extols the perfection of symmetries and laws,
many of which we do not yet know.
Their constancy allows us to divine God's faithfulness.

Yet these laws are not rigid.
Even in chance, God's will is carried out.

All things in the universe,
perhaps even the universe itself,
will wither, according to laws and to chance.
Death seems to rule the world.
But the new has also emerged,
that which never existed before. Unexpectedly,
new dimensions and forms could develop.
Out of Good Friday, God's grace let Easter happen.
In the despair of a great catastrophe,
something new arose, according to God's will.
This gives us hope by our own death
and for the future of the cosmos.

Each second which ticks, through our heart and
through the whole universe,
is a new creation.
It allows us to sense the proximity of the Creator
and the Creator's work.
In every moment, the old dies away,
the new arises, the world develops.
The presence of God is imprinted in time.
We can read about it in the book of evolution,
in which we ourselves form a chapter.

God's creation exceeds the knowledge
in our data banks.
If we approach God with reverence,
we become receptive
to the perfection of the laws,
open to the new that we encounter in Jesus,
and then the nearness of God in space and time
becomes known to us.

Let my images and forms be pleasing to You,
and let my innermost thoughts reach You,
God, my Center, and the Origin of the cosmos!

Figure 3: The Andromeda Galaxy (M31), 2.6 million light years distant, looks very similar to our own galaxy, the Milky Way. It contains three hundred billion (300,000,000,000) stars, which form a flat disk around a bright central bulge. Two dwarf galaxies circle the galaxy (Photo: Mount Palomar).

Conclusions

The concept of God is foreign to scientific perceptions and language. The scientific method postulates causality and requires objectivity; with such, God cannot be perceived. Nevertheless, "religious reason" may perceive a reflection of God's actions in nature—for example, in the constancy of natural laws that can bring forth something new, and in the ongoing creation of a new present, apparently out of nothing. Accordingly, one can understand the concept of creation today only as playing itself out not exclusively in the distant past, but as occurring throughout the entire development of the universe, here and now as well as in the distant future. This future consequence becomes important in relation to hope and is discussed in the last part of this book.

As we now focus on the beginning of the universe, the central question becomes: What is real? The answer depends on the methods by which one approaches this reality: whether as an objective, indifferent investigator or as an involved participant in the whole.

Part 2

PHYSICS AND REALITY

AN ASTRONOMICAL
BREATHING MEDITATION

As we breathe, we exchange substances essential for life; without breathing we could hardly live for a quarter of an hour. Our most important exchange activity is with air! Since I cannot see it, my mental image of air is limited. Even when I hear it during a storm, feel it on the skin, and sometimes smell it, it remains mysterious. Nothing changes when I know that it consists of an unimaginably great number of small molecules. For with the inner eye, I can only imagine a single molecule of air and this only figuratively. A nitrogen molecule, for example, has the form of two balls connected by steel springs: both nitrogen atoms which revolve around each other, swing lightly against one another and, every billionth of a second, collide with another molecule. Each of these unpretentious structures has an exciting past of many billions of years.

With a deep inhalation, I fill my lungs with about one liter of air. The gas of this volume of air consists of $3 \cdot 10^{22}$ freely moving, individual molecules. Three-fourths of them are nitrogen molecules and just about a quarter are similarly constructed oxygen molecules. The rest consists of water molecules, argon atoms, and a few rarer components. In around three hundred million lung vesicles, part of the oxygen is taken up by the blood and exchanged for carbon dioxide, a waste product of the metabolism. The nitrogen and the other components of the gas remain unaltered.

After the exhalation, the molecules from my lungs mix with those of the outside air. Measurements after atomic bomb explosions and reactor accidents have emphatically and alarmingly demonstrated how individual atoms from a single place on the globe can, with time, reach into the deepest corner of every house. Exactly in this manner, the exhaled molecules will be dispersed within a few years by the wind over the entire Earth. The Earth's atmosphere contains about 10^{44} molecules. When the exhaled molecules of a single draft of breath mix with the whole atmosphere, there are on the average ten of these per liter of air. According to the laws of chance, only in every hundredth liter of air is none of them present. The reaction-poor nitrogen molecules remain for millennia in the atmosphere and take part in everything that happens therein.

In every deep breath there must be a few molecules that I have pushed out with the first cry after my birth. In the same draft of air, I breathe in some that were present when Diogenes wished from the king: "Go away from the sun!" or some of those that Jesus exhaled in his last word: "It is accomplished."

Nitrogen and oxygen are not the material out of which the world originally consisted. As it was previously described, most of the elements in Earth's air formed through the nuclear fusion of helium in the glowing hot interior of old stars and, after millions of years, were shipped in stellar winds into interstellar space. There the hot gas cooled down to the temperature of space, a few degrees above absolute zero.[25] Dust and ice particles formed, which contained, among other things, oxygen and nitrogen. Now began the long journey, during which the dust mixed again with the original interstellar gas. It perhaps became a star with this gas again, and was once again expelled to reform itself, and so on, until some ice crystals, at the point of formation of the Earth, melted and evaporated—and finally after billions of years, oxygen and nitrogen became part of our atmosphere.

Still older are both hydrogen atoms which are part of every water molecule. Each formed out of a free electron and proton in the ionized plasma of the early universe. At about a half million years after the Big Bang, when the cosmic material cooled down to three thousand degrees, the electron-proton attraction stabilized into a hydrogen atom. With the phase transition from a plasma to a hydrogen gas, the universe became transparent all at once. Later the hydrogen atoms reacted with the oxygen of the first stars and formed water molecules.

Air contains the entire past of the universe. Through breathing, I feel myself bound to human as well as to cosmic history. I name this observation a meditation, because it involves the "I." In it, I encounter a reality that presupposes scientific findings but which, nevertheless, leads to quite different experiences that cannot be completely grasped in words.

RELATION BETWEEN SUBJECT
AND OBJECT

S ince the eighteenth century, science has had the reputation of being able to communicate a simple, mathematically describable reality. Contributing to this image is the fact that the complicated "I" of the human being is screened from this reality. Such exclusion is no longer completely possible today. In modern physics, which is based on quantum mechanics,[26] the relationship between the observing subject and the observed object is strangely entangled. The quantum world does not exist apart from the subject, for its reality is only created definitively through observation. This is a hard nut to crack that even the physicists have not yet completely absorbed. Yet today, the most important branches of technical work are unthinkable without quantum physics. Physical reality and its subject-object relationship represent the theme of this chapter.

Uncertainty in Quantum Mechanics

The reality of modern physics deals with uncertainty and the wave nature of matter. In quantum mechanics, elementary particles are not assumed to be tiny balls or points as in classical physics, but are described through a wave function. In the view of quantum mechanics, a particle is blurred to a diffuse little cloud. Surprisingly, the size and form of this cloud are not characteristics of the particle, but depend upon the experiment with which one observes the particle. The square of the wave function signifies the probability with which the particle finds itself at a certain position and at a given time, as Max Born showed already in 1926.

One finds the particle more often where this probability is great than at other locations. It cannot be predicted, however, where it will be at a certain point in time. In quantum mechanics, the future of a particle is not exactly fixed and mathematically determined as in classical mechanics. The future happening is given through the development of the wave function and only statistically determined. Although more than a half century old, this conclusion of quantum mechanics is as revolutionary today as it was then, for our thinking has remained largely classical.

As long as the particle is not observed, its wave function behaves mathematically like a wave in three-dimensional space. Niels Bohr described the concepts of wave and particle as complementary. Mathematically and technically they exclude each other, yet the image to be selected depends on the kind of experiment. Gamma rays and radio waves are, for example, physically the same as light, only with other wave lengths and other energies. One measures gamma rays with detectors and observes individual photons, which in this moment appear as pointlike particles. Radio waves, though, are measured technically more simply with receivers tuned to the waves. Similarly, radio interferometers can detect the same wave with telescopes that are placed at a distance thousands of kilometers apart. The same radio waves, however, appear also as single photons, if they, for example, hit a molecule with a diameter of a few ten-millionths of a millimeter, and set it to vibrate. What we consider the essence of a photon is ascertained only by observing it. It is senseless to speak of the wave or particle characteristic of a quantum object without relating the method of observation used to measure it.

The fact that the probability of a particle's location, called probability density, propagates in wave form, differentiates quantum reality from the classical view. The matter wave of a particle behaves like a wave on a lake. It is deflected at a wall, is reflected at an obstacle, spreads out spherically after moving through a hole, and can interfere with itself. These characteristics demonstrate that one is dealing with a real wave. The most important difference is that the classical surface waves of a lake never appear as particles. In our conception and in the classical physics of Newton, the characteristics of particles and waves are diametrically opposed.

How can electrons, then, simultaneously be particles and waves? In the Newtonian worldview, particles and waves belonged to an objective reality, even when one does not observe them. Yet according to the concept of wave-particle complementarity, the Copenhagen school of Bohr and Heisenberg concluded that, on the level of atoms and elementary particles, there exists no reality as long as we do not observe it. The quantum world is undefined and can only be described statistically until that time when we interfere with a measurement.

An important result of this are the *uncertainties* in position and momentum of a particle, which are not simultaneously measurable to arbitrary accuracy. Position and momentum are termed a conjugated pair. The more accurately the position is known, the more inaccurate is the momentum. Another conjugated pair are energy and time. The less time one has for the measurement, the less accurate is the determination of the energy. An evident basis for uncertainty is the wave nature of the probability density. The theory is, in this way, consistent with itself, for the means of observation are also uncertain. Just as a blind person searches a rolling ball with his hands, so the measuring instrument transmits an uncertain, unknown, small amount of energy. Even when we only observe an object, the information is transmitted by photons that consist of fuzzy wave packets, and a blurred image results. The smaller the examined object, the larger the influence of the uncertain research equipment, even if this only turns out to be photons. We do not cause the uncertainty, but with our observational equipment do take part in uncertainty. Since, without observation, we could not experience reality, uncertainty is unavoidable.

Quantum mechanics became in the course of the twentieth century the most capable tool available to science. It suppressed classical dynamics as the central discipline and is the unifying foundation of modern physics and chemistry. Never before had a single theory explained so many observational phenomena. Quantum uncertainty not only plays an important role in the realm of the most minute phenomena, it also claims a place in our lives. Quantum effects in living creatures are surprisingly common. Our hearing is limited by the quantum uncertainty of the tiny hairs on the receptor cells in the inner ear. The received signal is led over nerve fascicles that transmit electric signals by organic molecules, thanks to a quantum effect, and then is directed into the brain, where probably the majority of the processes are quantumlike. The Earth is constantly bombarded by energetic elementary particles from the cosmos. If a cosmic particle, after many collisions with atmospheric molecules, hits a gene from the germ cell of a living creature, the point of impact and, with it, the alteration and mutation are not predetermined. Uncertainty also plays a decisive role in the formation of germ cells, as the hereditary material from both parents is formed through chance processes into new gene combinations. Human existence is directly connected with the uncertainties and chance operations of the quantum world.

"God does not throw dice," objected Albert Einstein to the new physics, to which he himself initially had contributed greatly and for which he even received the Nobel Prize. He could not believe that genuine chance really exists. Yet the physical part of the statement, quantum uncertainty, was indeed corroborated. With Born's statistical interpretation of the wave function, physicists abandoned the mechanical model of the world and the clockwork paradigm. Nature in its minutest elements is hidden behind a curtain of uncertainties. We do not know what nature does behind this curtain, until, through an irreversible act of measurement, it is actualized. What we then perceive is a chance image. Nevertheless, chance has a system, for the mean values taken over many events behave deterministically and, in general, just as classical physics predicts.

A God who threw dice behind the curtain would be meaningless for the general case and would have to adhere strongly to the prescribed mean values. God is not needed for this purpose; every gambling machine can do it. Einstein wanted to make no theological statement, but to maintain that if quantum physics were correct, the world would be crazy. This actually appears to be the case.[27] As a classical physicist, Einstein was still convinced that the whole of reality must be, in the end, comprehensible. It is not, as Bohr and his successors demonstrated.

What Is Physical Reality?

The measurement procedure is the decisive step toward experiencing reality in the quantum world. After Niels Bohr and Werner Heisenberg, according to the so-called Copenhagen interpretation, the quantum world has no objectivity. It consists, until the point of observation, only of probabilities. *An event, a process, or even an object are only real if measured.* This concept necessitated the differentiation between observer and examined object. Where, however, is this dividing line, and who is the observer? When exactly is the object real? Is it when the computer reads the measurement device, when the scientists take cognizance of the measurements, or when outsiders hear about the results? The Copenhagen interpretation simply states that a differentiation between the observer and the observed object must be made, but does not say where this dividing line is positioned.

It is amazing that, concerning quantum mechanics, only the brilliant mathematical apparatus is really clear and has been well known since the end of the 1920s. Since then, it has surrendered millions of correct results without exception. It is only when mathematical formulas are translated into human language and concepts, like "object" and "subject," that puzzling problems of interpretation arise. It is unclear whether the theory is still incomplete in this issue or whether the quantum world is really absurd. Possibly both are the case. Such difficulties bring to mind the speechlessness of religious experiences.[28]

The Copenhagen interpretation explains the results of laboratory experiments, but makes no statement about the reality of the whole universe, including the observers. If one applied the Copenhagen interpretation to the universe, it would suggest that, without observing human beings, the cosmos does not really exist. This consequence, which even the Copenhageners did not carry so far, is not readily accepted by most physicists. Obviously one can also apply quantum theoretical methods to macroscopic objects, for instance, to cats. But when the question arises as to whether a cat still lives in a sealed box, one cannot answer in quantum mechanical terms: "There is half of a living and half of a dead cat inside, smeared through the whole box," as Erwin Schrödinger[29] once jestingly formulated. We are not allowed to imagine its quantum mechanical probability wave as an objective being, for without observation, the animal is not real for the questioning subject.

The reality of the cat in the box can be subsequently reconstructed objectively. If it is still living when the box is opened, it must have been breathing during the whole experiment. One can ascertain its past desire to eat by the amount of cat food left. If it is dead, perhaps the hour of death can be determined from the body temperature. For the flight of a single electron through a hole in the wall, the case is otherwise. It leaves behind no irreversible traces that can subsequently still be observed. Schrödinger's image is therefore no paradox, but a lesson as to how one can understand quantum reality. Consciousness does not call up reality. It is rather the observation, as an irreversible process, that transfers information from one object to another. Conversely, every irreversible step is in principle observable or traceable. Quantum mechanics indicates a close connection between irreversible time and objective reality. Reality demands as its tribute the irreversible march of time.

The most profound reason for quantum mechanical uncertainty lies in the fact that, on the one hand, a perceiving subject, sharply divided from the object, enters the physical scene while, on the other hand, subject and object cannot be sharply divided during an observation. Without uncertainty, quantum mechanics would contradict itself. The subject and its observational instruments are also, at this moment of interaction, parts of the quantum world. In the worldview of classical physics, the subject was not necessary to constitute the outside reality. According to the separation of subject and nature René Descartes had introduced in the seventeenth century, classical physics occupies itself solely with nature. In classical physics, reality exists also without a self-conscious subject. In quantum mechanics, though, subject and object must be brought into a direct, irreversible point of contact during the measurement procedure and must overcome the separation, so that something objective can be stated about reality. The separation of subject and object can never be wholly achieved.

As a result of uncertainty, a new element appears, *chance*. This is fully integrated into the physical worldview by virtue of the probability character of wave functions. Quantum mechanical chance is a part of the natural world and cannot be regarded as a crack in scientific reality through which we can directly see a sovereignly acting God shining forth. It will be explained later how the operation of chance in quantum events is bound to the rules of statistics.

In summary, we maintain that the physical world does not correspond to that paradigm of a flat, mechanical view of interlocking gears postulated earlier in the model of a clockwork universe. The world of the microcosmos imaged today in physics is not like a doll house, a reduced copy of the daily world. Its reality possesses a whole other structure. It is rich, diverse, and has a depth that was unsuspected earlier; it remains puzzling to us in many ways. The new view of scientific reality has a considerable influence on current ideas about the origin of the universe, as we shall see.

HOW MATERIAL IS MATTER?

I n addition to demolishing the classical separation of subject and object, modern physics has shaken still another supposed foundation of material reality. The atoms of modern science are, as is well known, not the indivisible building blocks of matter, as Democritus had thought. They consist of a nucleus and an outer shell of electrons, the most well-known kind of leptons.[30] The atomic nucleus is, as already known for a long time, composed of protons and neutrons. In recent years, experiments in large accelerators showed that these are not elementary particles, but that each consists of three quarks.[31] An interesting case is the neutral pion, which appears only for a short time during decays. Like all pions, the neutral pion consists of one quark and its antiquark, but they are each mixtures of two different quarks and antiquarks. Both quark-antiquark pairs constantly turn into each other, as energy, momentum, charge, and further so-called quantum numbers remain constant. What is perceived as a particle by measurement is the average of many processes. We are therefore brought to recognize that matter is not something static that remains forever, but is ever-changing. Matter can arise out of energy and again dissolve into energy. Matter sparkles, as an unsteady phenomenon, as variable as a chameleon. Time appears in all basic equations and is, consequently, a significant component of matter.

I observe an apple that apparently lies peacefully in my hand. If my eyes were a trillion (10^{12}) times sharper and could see a quintillion (10^{18}) times faster, the apple could be compared to a wasp's nest full of bubbling particles that form and then disappear again, whirl around as field quanta with the speed of light, or vibrate rhythmically against one another. If I bite into the apple, the bubbling goes further and unites with the hubbub in my body. What keeps this turmoil under control and holds up the world?

Particles and Field Quanta

Physical fields of force appear in quantum theory in the form of quanta. What however does a force have to do with quanta? If a particle repels another, a force originating with the first particle must have an effect at the location of the second particle. As energy is transmitted and, according to quantum theory, can only vary by leaps, the field of force must also be quantized. The field quanta remind me of the situation of two skaters standing opposite one another and throwing snowballs. The momentum that they transfer through this action forces them away from one another. Every throw brings them even faster apart and, in the temporal average, they feel the throws as a repelling force. The force consists of a number of individual quantum thrusts.

Field quanta cannot normally be detected directly. One therefore names them *virtual*. Only if something alters with the situation, for example, if a change moves abruptly, can a virtual quantum take up energy. From this moment on, it behaves like a normal particle and is real. It can thus be demonstrated with appropriate detectors. Best known field particles are photons, the quantized field of the electromagnetic force.

Analogous to the formation of real field quanta, particles can also originate from energy. Einstein's theory of special relativity shows that mass is a form of energy. Already in the 1930s, Paul Dirac connected the still young quantum mechanics with the theory of relativity. He found an equation for the electron that contains all the known characteristics of the particle. The equation, however, has a second solution for a practically identical particle with an opposite, positive charge. The positron, as it is called, was discovered by experimental physicists two decades later in cosmic rays, the particle radiation from space. Positrons are symmetrical in their electric charge to electrons.

The equations of the quantum field theory are so fashioned that, for every particle, there must be a mirror image with the opposite charge. This symmetry of nature goes even significantly further. When new particles originate from energy, they must always appear in pairs, since for every charge there must also be created its opposite. The theories of elementary particles require that the sum of all charges—positive minus negative—in the entire universe remains constant. Nature, in this regard, is surprisingly conservative. This property has already been confirmed experimentally on numerous occasions. Along with the charge, there are other quantum numbers, whose total sum likewise does not change in the course of time. Symmetry and conservation requirements rule the quantum world and represent the deepest insights of the human mind into the microcosmos.

Properties of the very smallest things have practical significance when considering events in the early universe and the origin of matter. But we must first appreciate the character of that condition without matter, the vacuum.

The Vacuum Is Not Nothing

Except for their uncertainty, elementary particles and field quanta have no measurable expansion. One could now conjecture that, with the exception of these singular points, space contained substantially nothing. How incorrect! The vacuum, as this empty space in physics is called, is in permanent flux, where all particles and field quanta of nature incessantly form and disappear. *By definition, a vacuum is the lowest state of energy left when everything in space is removed that can be removed.* The natural laws cannot be removed. Therefore there always remains in a quantum vacuum a certain amount of energy left over on account of the unavoidable virtual particles. One does not yet know the value of energy at the zero point of empty space. Whether the zero-point energy originated with the universe or whether it first came about through radiation from quantum fluctuations during the course of time are open to conjecture. Since its absolute value is not yet measurable, the zero-point energy remains very puzzling.

What is certain is that the zero-point energy, like every other form of energy, is uncertain and fluctuates in space and time. Heisenberg's uncertainty principle states that a fluctuation must have a duration that is the shorter, the greater the energy is. By our daily, macrocosmic standards, fluctuations are stupendously fast. Even the energy of the tiny mass of one electron appears for only 10^{-20} seconds. The ratio of this time to one second is smaller than one second is in proportion to the present age of the universe. One might imagine the energy fluctuations as chaotic fluctuations on the water surface of a swimming pool. The zero-point energy corresponds to the average water mark, and locations of elevated energy are similar to the wave crests. The excess energy can transform itself within a short time into particles, conforming to the laws of quantum field theory. In accord with the symmetries of elementary particle physics, particles and antiparticles always form in pairs. Within the temporal uncertainty, they must disappear again to comply with the laws of conservation of energy. They never last long enough to be detectable. Nature has arranged it so that one can never observe such particles directly. The particle pairs are like cavorting dolphins in the ocean: when one finally has the camera at the ready, they have disappeared again. Such particles are named virtual, analogous to virtual field quanta.

Does this tumultuous chaos of energy, virtual particles, and field quanta really exist then? The energy of the vacuum was first demonstrated in 1958 by the Dutch physicist J. M. Sparnaay in the Casimir effect. His compatriot Hendrick Casimir had predicted a force that presses two metal plates together in a vacuum. The zero-point energy, apart from its fluctuations, is distributed homogeneously and present in every cubic centimeter of space. Between the plates, certain wavelengths of virtual vacuum photons are suppressed so that the zero-point energy and its associated pressure are smaller there. The pressure difference actually presses the plates against each other.

There are also indirect indications in the spectral lines of atoms that the distribution of electrons around the atomic nucleus is slightly disturbed by the presence of virtual particles. Their shadowy dance has real consequences. They give out an even more impressive display when external energy is fed in—for example, in the form of an accelerated particle striking a stationary particle. Virtual particles can then suddenly become real particles (Fig. 4) that are no longer bound to the temporal uncertainty of the vacuum and can be demonstrated in particle detectors. In this manner the top-quark was recently discovered.

Real existing, normal particles also have characteristics that are reminiscent of the bubbling vacuum. For a short time, they can decay into several particles or field quanta. The new particles are virtual and reunite again soon into the original particle, so that the energy in the temporal average remains constant. It is this energy that makes the difference between real and virtual particles. Real particles jut out permanently from the ocean of zero-point energy. Although they themselves change roles

Figure 4: The nucleus of a sulfur atom was shot with high energy into a gold foil. The impact created an avalanche of new particles. They originated from the sea of virtual states (Photo: CERN).

like actors, these islands of reality persist. The law of energy conservation and other symmetries prevent their sinking back into the ocean of the vacuum. They bring order from the turmoil and guarantee reality.

Why is energy conserved? Why doesn't the world sink back into the virtual sea of the vacuum? These questions exceed the scope of quantum field theory. The hypothetical possibilities that come to mind here originate instead from human experiences of crisis and correspond to anxieties over extinction. Answering the questions above with a "God hypothesis" might also exceed the experience of faith, for God could then become an undemonstrable, metaphysical power without any relation to the questioner. It is, however, just this relation that constitutes faith. I find the remark of Carl Friedrich von Weizsäcker the most apt: "Physics does not explain away the secrets of nature, it refers these back to deeper underlying secrets."[32]

THE BEGINNING OF THE UNIVERSE

M any physicists suppose that the origin of the world has something to do with particle conservation in the microcosmos. The very large and the very small encountered each other in the Big Bang about fourteen billion years ago, when the universe began its expansion from a small, immeasurably dense volume. All real elementary particles and all energy in the universe were concentrated in the smallest space. The gigantic masses of whole galaxies, which today are millions of light years away from each other, still lay within the proximity of a thousandth millimeter. Also present was kinetic energy in the form of cosmic expansion of the galaxies. A third important form was gravitational energy. According to Newton, it always has a negative sign and increases toward zero if two masses distance themselves from each other. It is remarkable that the computed negative gravitational energy in the universe today approximately cancels the positive energies from matter and expansion. The balance is reconciled within the margin of inaccuracy; the total energy of the universe is consistent with zero.

Did the universe originate from a condition devoid of energy? Can the vacuum or even nothingness give birth to a universe? Before we examine this preposterous hypothesis, we must return once again to gravitation. From the standpoint of quantum field theory, it is a shrill anachronism to apply Newton's theory of gravitation from the seventeenth century. In the present theory of gravity, the general theory of relativity formulated by Albert Einstein in 1917, it is not so easy to specify the gravitational energy of the universe. Relative to the present value, it was surely smaller in the early universe—one can calculate exactly how much smaller—and perhaps also negative, but its absolute sum is not defined. The general theory of relativity is nevertheless hardly the conclusive theory of gravitation. For general relativity is the only branch of contemporary physics that is not yet quantum-mechanically decoded. Observations in celestial mechanics, particularly of pulsars in binary systems, have readily confirmed the general theory of relativity. Even so it is very doubtful whether this classical theory, which preceded quantum mechanics, would also be valid under the extreme conditions of the early phase of the Big Bang. Considering the limitations of general relativity, it should be clear that the following statements are very speculative. It is really not important here whether the details are correct; it is worth noting, however, that one can conceive of scientific explanations at all.

The Vacuum Hypothesis

The possibility that the total energy of the universe is zero has given impetus to the vacuum hypothesis.[33] Accordingly, the whole universe originated from a fluctuation in the primeval vacuum. One of many possibilities, for example, would be that two particles, let's name them "cosmons," could have originated each with half of the mass of the entire universe, including more than 10^{49} tons visible in the stars. The energy of the cosmons' mass could have exactly equaled the negative energy of their opposed gravity, so that the balance of energy was even. Because, then, the total energy came to zero, the original fluctuation of the vacuum could have persisted infinitely long. The idea of cosmons has already been suggested by various scientists, among others by A. Salam. It touches on the speculation that quarks and leptons arose from more energetic particles, which had likewise formed from the decay of particles still richer in energy, and so on.

Please note: cosmons are purely hypothetical and not a generally sanctioned physical concept. There are neither theoretical hints nor observed indications. Cosmons would be even more elementary than quarks and leptons, into which they proceeded to decay.

The origin of the universe out of a vacuum could be likened to the establishment of a business without any financial resources. The entrepreneur borrows money from a bank. He signs a promissory note and receives a check for it. With this capital, he buys a factory, a house, and everything that he needs to live. From the profit from his undertaking he pays for his living expenses and for the bank interest. Although he initially had nothing and also later his net worth just about balances his debts, his taxable worth being zero, he does have the necessary material goods. It is likewise imaginable that the universe could have "borrowed" energy against gravitation during a fluctuation in the primary vacuum. The universe could have originated similarly, without a supply of energy and still today have a total energy of zero.

The primary vacuum is difficult to imagine, since there was no surrounding matter that could serve as a reference for position and time. Without an object that could be applied as a standard or a process from which a time could be derived, space and time cannot be defined. Physically, it makes no sense to speak of a time before the first particles span space and time through their real existence. Space and time first originated in the Big Bang. The primary vacuum, therefore, cannot be described like a *present* vacuum, in which space and time determine the uncertainties of momentum and energy. Nevertheless, the primary vacuum must have already contained all the physics of the later universe. According to these laws, the formation of matter then proceeded to unfold.

It follows from the vacuum hypothesis that the universe did not originate from nothing. It is not provable but imaginable that the physical laws of conservation and symmetries were preexistent. Since there was neither space nor time, the laws could only have had a latent existence. As soon as the primary fluctuation occurred, the universe formed pursuant to the presently valid laws.

Virtual particles arise spontaneously in a vacuum according to the rules of pure chance, but with calculable probability. If the universe arose in an analog manner, there would have been no cause for it. What the first cause was that produced an effect and thus started the clock of causality to tick may remain hidden behind the veil of quantum uncertainty, perhaps forever.

Where now does God enter the picture of the origin of the universe? Nowhere forcibly. On the causal level of scientific explanations, God does not figure on principle. There are still undoubtedly many serious gaps in our knowledge, but none hints at an explanation that necessarily lies outside science. From the seventeenth century on and even today, natural laws have often been elevated metaphysically and presented as creation ideas of God.[34] However, not even a mathematically formulated natural law can claim absolute validity. The development of science, particularly of physics, has produced many examples of how such laws have ended up as approximations of a later theory. An empirically obtained natural law can therefore claim no absolute truth. Nevertheless, I reckon that from the perspective of religious faith, one can perceive a masterful creator in such laws that have brought forth a universe, even though these laws are only partially and approximately known. One can derive no proof of God from such, but may instead understand the relationship a cognizant human being bears to God and the world. One might also learn how to deepen this relationship and make it understandable to others.

Dark Matter: More Important Than Expected

Aristotle (384–322 B.C.) knew that the Earth was round and was already approximately familiar with the Earth's circumference. He estimated it at 400,000 stadia. A Greek stadium is about 150 meters long. Aristotle could then calculate that his Greek Mediterranean world with a radius of about 2,000 kilometers encompasses a few percent of the Earth's surface. The rest must have been for him a world full of mysteries and inexhaustible possibilities. It is quite similar with us in today's universe. Only that cosmic matter which emits sufficient light, X-rays, or radio waves can be directly observed. This is termed *visible matter*. It includes stars, atomic hydrogen gas, hot plasma, and energetic electrons. Too dim and not visible for us are distant comets, planets, cold white dwarfs, black holes, and perhaps particles and objects not yet known to us at present. They form the *dark matter*. In the following, evidence will be presented suggesting that the quantity of dark matter far exceeds that of visible matter.

The temporal duration of the revolution of a star around the galactic center depends solely upon the radius of the orbit and the mass encircled by the orbit, including visible as well as dark matter. Revolution time and radii of orbits can be measured in the Milky Way as well as in neighboring galaxies and from such data, the total mass can be determined. It is concluded from the Sun's course in the galaxy that the encircled mass must be slightly larger than what one estimates, based on visible stars and gas clouds. Farther out in the Milky Way, and similarly in other galaxies, the discrepancy increases quickly. Furthermore, the mass of galaxies operates on light and radio waves like a lens. The power of deflection is a further measure for dark matter and points to a factor between five and ten of the visible mass. The orbital motion of some binary galaxies can only be explained by there being twenty times more mass present therein than the visible objects amount to. In clusters of galaxies, values thirty times as large were determined. Apparently there resides plenty of dark matter between the galaxies.

Dark matter is noticeable through its gravity (Fig.5). Of particular interest is the question whether this force is sufficient to stop or even to reverse the general expansion of the universe, ongoing since the Big Bang. It would take an average mass density of over $5 \cdot 10^{-24}$ grams per cubic meter, dispersed over the entire universe, or approximately the mass of three hydrogen atoms per cubic meter, to accomplish this. This *critical density* is a million times smaller than that in the space between us and the nearest stars. Let us imagine a hollow sphere with a radius ten times that of Earth. In order to fill it with air having critical density, the atoms one breathes out in a single exhalation would suffice.

Nevertheless the visible matter—on the average over the entire universe—amounts to only a small percentage of the critical density. Outside the galaxies, in enormously huge spaces, there is hardly one single visible atom in the volume of a room. It can be stated with great certainty that there is ten times more mass present in the universe than we can currently see and recognize. What the dark matter consists of is the big question. Many forms are possible. Suggestions include protostars that could not develop into stars, planetlike heavenly bodies, molecular hydrogen gas, black holes, neutrinos, still unknown elementary particles, and last but not least, the zero-point energy of the vacuum which, like all energy, also corresponds to a mass.

Speculation, however, is increasingly limited by observations. For example, we can now rule out the possibility that critical density is reached through normal matter from protons and neutrons, since otherwise more helium and lithium would have fused in the early universe than are observed today. The upper limit density of normal matter amounts to about 5 to 10 percent of the critical value. Additional matter would have to consist of elementary particles like neutrinos or of hypothetical exotics, such as the unproven axions or strings that had formed in the Big Bang.

Already in 1930, Wolfgang Pauli postulated the neutrino to interpret a nuclear decay process. Without this postulate, energy would not be conserved in the process. The new particle was extremely difficult to detect since it has no charge. Pauli computed the mass as being "small to the

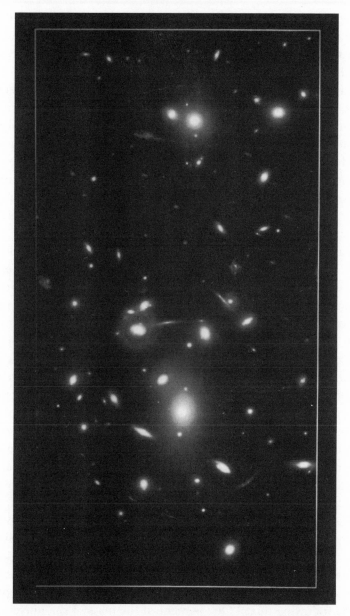

Figure 5: Clusters of galaxies are the largest stable and probably the oldest structures in the universe. The cluster Abell 2218 in the picture has a diameter of a hundred million light years. All of the diffuse flecks are distant galaxies, the circular structures are deflections of the light from even more remote galaxies in the gravity field of the cluster (Photo: NASA).

point of vanishing." It is still today not definitely acknowledged, but is presumably less than a millionth of the mass of an electron, which is itself less than a thousandth of a proton. The interaction of neutrinos with matter is therefore extremely weak.

A neutron can fly through many atoms and even atomic nuclei without leaving any trace. In order to reduce the particle flux of a neutrino beam to one half, a block of lead with the depth of about one hundred light years would be required. Neutrinos belong to the family of leptons and probably originated in great numbers in the early universe. They uncoupled one second after the beginning, and since then, they fly practically unhindered through the cosmos almost with the speed of light. If they actually have mass, they could contribute substantially to the dark matter of the universe.

The thesis that the zero-point energy of the vacuum contributes to the mass and gravity of the universe must also be taken seriously. Zero-point energy would then have the function of a "cosmological constant." Albert Einstein had introduced this quantity at a time before cosmic expansion was known, in order to explain why the universe does not collapse under its own gravitation. To make a significant, but not overwhelming contribution to the energy of the universe, the energy density of the vacuum must be about a ten-thousandth of the solar radiation which hits the Earth. Why the vacuum would have exactly this energy remains puzzling, though.

From far off objects whose light only reaches us at this moment, astronomers can observe directly how galaxies originated in the intergalactic gas of the early universe. The formation is also simulated with computer models. They show that only in a universe with close to the critical density could galaxies emerge in the observed time of a billion years. Certain assumptions about the composition of matter and energy in the universe must be made for the observed distribution in clusters of galaxies and other large structures to occur. These models also permit inferences as to the amount and kind of dark matter. The indications one gets from all present observations and simulations may be reproduced with the following mix.[35] One percent of the mass of the universe is visible; a few percent are invisible, but consist of normal matter; neutrinos and other elementary particles comprise a fifth; the energy of the vacuum may contribute to the rest, about three-fourths.

The possibility that the cosmos consists primarily of zero-point energy or still unknown particles is a serious possibility. Both would have little interaction with normal matter and could slumber unnoticed in our body or cross through the Earth. Nevertheless they would be a part of our reality, for they would have played a decisive role in the formation of the galaxies. It is humbling to note that until recently, we have probably observed and examined only a small percentage of the cosmic matter. Thus far, we may have seen of the universe much less than the proverbial tip of the iceberg.

Developments in the Early Universe

At the conclusion of this chapter on the universe as a whole, contemporary ideas in physics about the early universe are briefly summarized. The reader should recognize that in this area of cosmology, physics itself, not only the models, remains speculative. Much is now being written about the early universe: the theories become more and more detailed as well as more numerous. They perhaps contribute less to the subject of faith and science than one would hope. What is offered in the following section, then, is a taste, rather than an exhaustive description, of these theories.

According to the general theory of relativity, every concentration of energy warps space so that, for example, light rays are deflected. The passage of time also varies and is treated by the same theory as a fourth dimension. In the immense concentration of energy in the early universe, the curvature was strong and in the smallest of spaces. Since, according to Heisenberg, energy and momentum are uncertain, the curvature of space and time in these tiny spaces must also be fluctuating and uncertain. Thus the space-time system of the general theory of relativity is invalid up until the Planck time, about 10^{-43} seconds after the beginning. There are already various theories to account for what happened within this time frame. We have become familiar with one of them, based on cosmons. Ed Tryon had the universe start right off with the present rate of expansion. Alex Vilenkin inserted an inflationary phase. James Hartle and Steven Hawking developed a model without a boundary in space and time by introducing an imaginary time, thereby skirting the singularity of the beginning.

More agreement reigns over the second phase, the *inflation*, that occurred at the latest after 10^{-34} seconds, but lasted for 10^{-33} seconds. When the temperature sank under the critical value of 10^{28} degrees, the state of the universe changed like water when it freezes. Prior to inflation, all of the physical forces in the universe, except for gravity, were equally strong and all particles similar. This symmetry broke. After the inflationary phase, the forces differed from each other and the antimatter disappeared, at least in our part of the universe. The natural laws remained unchanged and yet the universe comprised a new material content. The enormous energy of the released "melting heat" at the phase transition accelerated cosmic expansion at an unimaginable rate. The inflation bloated the universe by more than the factor of 10^{50}. Even after the inflationary phase, the whole presently observable universe had a diameter of only ten centimeters. In contrast, the expansion factor of 10^{27}, accounting for the elapsed fourteen billion years of normal cosmic expansion from the ten centimeters to the present size, appears almost modest.

What is interesting about the apparently bizarre theories of the inflationary period are their observable aftereffects in the present universe. The striking isotropy and the more or less uniform distribution of clusters of galaxies in space follow naturally from the idea that they are descended from a small region. The phenomenon of inflation is also the reason for the still relatively high temperature of the cosmos, three degrees over absolute zero. There is furthermore the important prediction, not yet confirmed through observations, that the average energy density of the universe is precisely critical. This would mean that the present expansion of the universe continues infinitely, but slows down due to its own gravitation. After an infinite period of time, it will come to a standstill.

Development after the inflation is already pretty well known. The universe was an almost homogeneous mixture of various kinds of quarks, leptons, and the field particles of the forces: a so-called *quark-gluon plasma*. It expanded according to the standard Big Bang model. When energetic particles produced by the largest accelerators on Earth collide head on, they release approximately the energy density of matter during the quark-gluon phase. Such experiments have allowed us to study some important processes of this phase in observable objects.

After a few millionths of a second, three quarks united to a proton or a neutron. Once again the universe changed fundamentally, and its components were the building blocks of the present atoms. They obeyed a physics similar to that of the relatively well understood core of stars. Protons and neutrons had about three minutes' time to fuse into helium and lithium in a universal *nucleosynthesis*. These are the same processes that today release energy inside a star. The conditions at the Big Bang were critical: if the universe had been less hot than about one billion degrees or denser than about 10^{27} of its present density, all matter would have become helium. The expansion of the universe interrupted further nucleosynthesis just at the right moment. The primordial matter in today's universe, 27 percent of which is composed of helium, is therefore an important indicator of the conditions in this phase. The rest of the cosmic matter remained as protons and electrons.

Around a half million years after the Big Bang, matter was cold enough for the formation of atoms out of protons and helium ions on the one hand, and electrons on the other. Atomic gas absorbs light and radio waves far less than the charged particles of preceding eras. The universe became transparent all of a sudden, so that today we can observe its further development from this moment in time. The expansion of the universe was now uncoupled from the radiation pressure and since then proceeds in ballistic fashion. The motion of cosmic material is determined by the momentum of motion and by gravity. In slightly overdense regions, the universe expanded somewhat slower and fell more and more behind until the region finally began to collapse. These regions attracted one another, collided, and combined to the present clusters of galaxies and to individual galaxies. The first stars formed.

The beginning was not like lifting a curtain to reveal all properties of the universe gathered at once on stage. The early universe should be seen rather as a phase of multitudinous creativity in cosmic dimensions, as fascinating and exciting as the later development of stars and planets portrayed previously.

WHY THIS UNIVERSE?

Why is the universe created in such a way that life is possible? A great number of conditions were necessary for prebiotic and biological development on the young Earth. The conditions in the early universe until the formation of the Sun's accretion disk, from the correct mix of primeval oceans with the minerals of primeval rock to the ideal temperature, resulting from Earth's most favorable distance from the Sun—all of these properties required quantitative values within a minimal percentile in order for evolution to proceed the way it actually did. The rotation of the Earth, the rhythm of day and night, the seasonal ebb and flow caused by the large moon of Earth, and even plate tectonics may have contributed to evolution. The Earth's magnetic field, which shields energetic elementary particles, and much more were indispensable. In narrow binary star systems, no small planets such as Earth ever form. Large outer planets with the size of a Jupiter are also necessary, since they divert comets and planetary fragments that constantly penetrate the inner solar system from outside. Large planets break them up or capture them so that inner planets like the Earth remain largely protected from them. Yet the bombardment of comets and asteroids upon the Earth was not absent, and it played a critical role in evolution. Such catastrophes apparently occurred in just the right measure.

Naturally, life can only originate in a location conducive to it. The many known conditions of life—new ones are identified each year—reveal an amazing interweaving of the necessary threads from biology, chemistry, astronomy, and physics. Most of the essential conditions on the planetary level appear to be chance coincidences. They could be considered as selection criteria: other planets and planet systems did not fulfill these conditions and did not become birthplaces of life. Such selection criteria define the life-engendering conditions of our Earth and planet system. If they were more precisely known, one could then estimate the abundance—more like the rarity—of the appearance of life in the universe.

Fine Tuning of the Universe

Those conditions which affect the entire universe contain another quality. Already in 1957, the American physicist Robert H. Dicke noticed that certain basic physical constants like elementary electrical charge, mass of protons, gravitational constant, and Planck's constant are not arbitrary quantities, for only at the observed values is life as we know it possible at all in the universe. Were the electron, for instance, as massive as its sister particle, the muon, the universe would consist of nothing but neutrons and neutrinos. There is still no explanation of why even one of these constants must be precisely what it is.

Another well-known example of the fine tuning of the universe is the generation of carbon from helium in old stars. This requires three helium nuclei per nucleus of carbon. That exactly three collide in the same moment is very improbable. Much more likely is the collision of two, which produces beryllium. The collision of a beryllium nucleus with a further helium nucleus does not necessarily yield a carbon nucleus, for in most collisions, the target is destroyed or just diverted. What's more—since beryllium only has a lifetime of 10^{-17} seconds—many attempts are not possible. Nevertheless beryllium fuses with helium to carbon because the carbon nucleus has a fortunate property. A resonance at precisely the correct value allows energy to radiate away very quickly. In the brief collision time during which beryllium and helium are together, the product emits two gamma quanta according to the energy levels of the carbon nucleus. After that, beryllium and helium no longer possess enough energy to exist as a single nucleus and must remain conjoined as carbon. Without this characteristic, which solely depends upon elementary constants and for which there is no explanation, no heavy elements could have formed in the aftermath. Organic chemistry, based on carbon, as well as life as we know it, would not exist.

The succeeding element, oxygen, also has a resonance. Fortunately, it lies about one percent too low. Otherwise most of the carbon would turn into oxygen and hence would be unavailable for planet formation and the development of life. Are the laws of nuclear physics intentionally planned with regard to the consequences in stellar evolution and to the development of the universe?[36]

As a third example among many others, one could mention the strange coincidence that the duration of biological evolution until the origin of intelligent life amounted to about half of the duration of the Sun's life. This particular time during which a star with the Sun's mass is stable and shines almost uniformly is given by physical constants determining the equilibrium and energy supply. Yet the biological speed of evolution depends on the rate of chemical reactions, astronomical cycles, frequency of bombardment by comets, the duration of biological generations, and much more, all of which could be different by orders of magnitude. If the mean period of evolution for intelligent life were considerably less than a billion years, it would have originated much earlier on the Earth; if it were much longer, the development would not have proceeded to the emergence of human beings before our central star was extinguished.

The Anthropic Principle

The apparent fine tuning of the universe to the benefit of humanity stimulated the English cosmologist Brandon Carter in 1974 to make the following warning: "What we can expect to observe must be restricted by the conditions necessary for our presence as observers."[37] To put it more simply: *That we can wonder at all that the universe is as it is, it must be exactly as it is, for otherwise we would not be here to wonder.* This so-called anthropic principle proceeds from the tenet that the human being is part of the universe and has originated according to natural laws. It reminds us that, as for any observation, the limits of the measurement apparatus (in this case the observer himself) must be taken into consideration. Historically, the anthropic principle was formulated just at the time when it became clear to astrophysicists that the universe had a beginning and that evolution began with the Big Bang. The observed coincidences are a priori conditions for the possibility of biological evolution. They must have been given before we could perceive the world at all. Certain physical, chemical, and biological characteristics are required through them. The

anthropic principle is yet no explanation of the cosmological coincidences. As established fact that must be fulfilled by any acceptable model
of the universe, it is a triviality. The anthropic principle, however, makes
one conscious of how strongly human existence is grounded in the whole
of the cosmos and what consequences follow as a result of this participation for our theoretical cognition.

To explain coincidences on the level of the whole universe, there appear to be three possibilities:

1. There are physical reasons which we still do not understand why
   the universe must be exactly as it is (the *causal* explanation).
2. There are many universes. We inhabit one that has the correct
   characteristics for evolution and for life (the *selective* explanation).
3. The universe is given a direction, the goal of which is to create life
   (the *teleological* or purpose-oriented explanation).

The usual methodology of modern science proceeds from what is observed, and seeks a causal explanation. Cosmologists receive their salary
with the commission of finding physical reasons. The rules of their trade
oblige them to seek causal explanations. In the twenty years or so since
Carter's publication, some coincidences of serious import have been interpreted. For instance, isotropy and homogeneity of the cosmos result
naturally from the inflationary model of the universe. Certain new, finely
tuned parameters have consequently come to light, however. In view of
this medusalike multiplication of coincidences, some researchers have
lost the patience or the courage to find a completely causal model. They
seriously weigh both of the other possibilities, despite their methodological hesitation.

With the selective explanation, the anthropic principle becomes a selection criterion among many universes with random characteristics.
Each of these universes would have other basic constants and other conditions at the beginning. Their totality would perhaps be an infinite en-
semble of universes. According to the definition of the term "universe,"
we could, however, observe no other except our own. Postulating en-
tities that are not observable by definition has led in the past to false
conclusions. A well-known example is the cosmic ether proposed as the
propagation medium for electromagnetic waves. It became superfluous
through the theory of special relativity and was then irrevocably ex-
punged. Although imaginable, the real existence of other universes is

fundamentally unprovable. The extension of the sciences beyond our reality into other, unobservable universes is therefore a step in the metaphysical direction, from which a number of experts turn away on principle.

The teleological explanation (*telos* Greek = end, goal, purpose) introduces a structure of finality into science. It has been taken into serious consideration, even though it is largely rejected and has unleashed much emotion in the camp of rationalistic scholarship. The new law would ascribe a tendency to the cosmos that enables life to come about, similar to the characteristic of constant energy. Different from energy conservation, for which no scientifically proven exception is known apart from temporary quantum effects, this character of finality would only guarantee the necessary conditions for life and would not be compelling. It seems unlikely that this view will ever find the kind of consensus other natural laws enjoy in physics.

Nevertheless, finality is not a stranger to the analytical structure of otherwise causal physics. The second law of thermodynamics contains finality with an assertion pointing to the future—the increase in entropy—without citing a causal basis. Self-organizing processes have an attractor or a goal toward which they independently set a course. It gives them a direction, toward which the causal microprocesses line up. Finality does not contradict causality[38] and does not exonerate science from the task of finding the individual causal events.

God as Power of Nature, God of the Gaps or Transcendence?

It is often assumed that a tendency toward finality would immediately imply a planning, purposefully acting providence. This conclusion is by no means inevitable. In any case, the third possibility for the explanation of the apparent fine tuning of the universe should neither be postulated as a scientific proof of God, nor opposed as such. Similarly, there is no causal explanation for other basic principles like, for instance, the conservation of energy. The lack of a causal explanation would not make God necessary. To postulate God because of it would be a metaphysical artifice similar to the suggestion that there is a huge number of unobservable universes.

To evoke God as cause where science still has no answer would presuppose a certain image of God. In such a line of thought, God is regarded as the immediate origin of certain things or events. This would bring God into a direct relationship with a natural power or a natural process. God would actually be a part of the process and of objectively perceivable nature. In this view, God would stand on the same level as the electrical force, for example, which pushes two equally charged bodies away from each other. In the language of modern science, which operates without the hypothesis of God as a general principle, a tendency toward finality should not be named "God," but rather a "natural characteristic of the universe."

Neither does the concept of God as a natural force correspond to the understanding of Judeo-Christian theology. Monotheism does not just consist of postulating a single God instead of many divinities. Above all, the monotheistic divine is not to be directly identified with the many objects and processes in nature. Because the divine transcends nature and thus appears as a unity, there can only be a single God in this view. The biblical creation stories turn expressly away from the deification of natural forces or processes. It is precisely this misidentification of the term "God" with a natural force in the causal view of the universe that many modern theologians vehemently oppose.

From the image of God as a hypothesis that is invoked when science cannot explain something, it is not a far step, then, to a God who exists solely in the gaps. Such a God, fixated and reduced to ever-present puzzling gaps in knowledge and bewildering coincidences, can be confidently set aside. God would be something like a watchmaker, who becomes insignificant as soon as a watch is purchased.

The watchmaker notion of God is not the only possibility. The ancient Hebrews and early Christians believed in quite another God, who does not dwell in the gaps, but functions rather in the present and the future. In the relation of the *biblical* God to fine tuned coincidences, the question is not whether *God* commanded them but rather *why* God has created everything, even the causally explainable between the gaps in our knowledge. It is not what is scientifically special—the exceptions, the gaps in knowledge, or coincidences—that particularly points to God. God appears rather in the perception that is prepared to listen, to wait patiently, and to enter into a relationship full of consequences. The biblical God says in the burning bush: "I am who I am." In that story,[39] one is told of very unusual circumstances: a fire in the wilderness whereby nothing burns up. The heart of the story concerns Moses' commission to lead the Israelites out of Egypt. God will be with them, and certainly not in burning bushes or other inexplicable miracles, but in the daily struggle to survive. From the biblical point of view, the ordinary is also full of enigmas and wonderment, for God acts behind humans and nature. God stands behind everything and is in everything transcendent.

In sum, science has found no divine fingerprints, by which the creator could be identified unmistakably. Therefore, if one speaks of God in nature, the term must be precisely explained and critically evaluated. The divine "stand-in" and the metaphysical elevation of the fine tuning of the universe or of the natural laws as "the thoughts of God" are two highly doubtful concepts when expressed in the language of science.

Yet there is another concept of God's connection with creation. It is based on the perception of a person related to nature, a relationship that allows for consequences in feeling, acting, and hope. We do not yet understand the fine tuning of the universe and should not set too much value on it. However, it may render us more apt to perceive divine action in everyday life, which sometimes appears similarly fine tuned.

In the following section, the origin of the new, but also of its opposite, decay, and the concept of creation will be discussed mainly from the perspective of biological development. The exposition is not meant to be exhaustive. I would far rather show how the biotic world developed according to the same laws as astrophysics, but with numerous, astoundingly imaginative variations.

Part 3

LIVING
AND
DYING

LIFE AT THE POND

There is a small pond in our garden, surrounded by willows and reeds. In the warm part of the year, grass-green water-frogs sun themselves on the wide leaves of water lilies. The amphibians, to which the frogs belong, are pioneers in the animal world. About 400 million years ago, they climbed out of the water and conquered the land for new living space. The great invention of these descendants of fish was to absorb oxygen from the air, which sea algae and later also a luxuriant plant world consisting of giant ferns and horsetails had produced over billions of years. Admittedly, the frogs have never quite broken away from the damp world of their forbears; their eggs still require constant moisture. Their larvae, the tadpoles, find their nourishment only in water. If one tiptoes to the pond, one can see the black-dotted creatures always on the sunniest leaves. The leaves sink under the weight of the largest so deeply that the frogs themselves are half underwater.

A dragonfly sits on a blade in the sun. Now and then it flies silently and jerkily over the water's surface and between the canes. If a rival appears in its territory, the opponents swarm over the water's surface, collide with an audible rustling and beating of wings, and chase one another until they are out of eyesight. Seconds later, the victor of the hunting ground reappears, as if nothing had happened. When landing on a blade, the dragonfly alights so softly that the blade remains motionless.

The water lies quietly, and on a warm summer's day, one has the impression that nothing happens here. Almost unnoticeably, a small pointed object pushes through the water's surface every ten minutes. It is the rear portion of a larva of the great water beetle, who fills its tracheal system with air. One can hardly see the slim larva, about as long as a match, under the water's surface. Only the catlike head makes the dark figure stand out. The larvae are elegant and rapid swimmers. In the course of evolution, they have developed mandibles from the upper jaw of early insects to deadly tongs, injection needles, and suction tubes. With these powerful weapons, the larva impales its victims—tadpoles and small frogs, fishes that are many times bigger than it is, or even larvae of its own kind—holds them tight, and injects a digestive enzyme. Enzymes effect chemical reactions without being used up themselves and thus are ideal chemical warfare agents. The poison dissolves the tissue until the inside of the prey is completely liquid and is digested, until it is only held together by skin. The larva then sucks the juice through his mandibles and leaves the empty shell behind. Larvae metamorphose into beetles that are no less rapacious. Another name for them is water tigers. In certain areas of Asia, these beetles are bred and sold as food; children especially like these beetles apparently as crisp treats.

One hardly sees the four wings of the dragonfly when it remains effortlessly still in the air waiting for prey. It recognizes a mosquito or small fly a hundred times faster than the human brain and hunts it down at a speed of up to a hundred kilometers per hour. It shreds a victim while still in the air with its sharp mouthpiece and endlessly cleans its faceted eyes with the forelegs after the meal.

Frogs, on the contrary, eat their booty whole. Lightning fast, they jump in the air to a height of up to ten times their length, enclose the victim with their sticky tongue, and swallow it. There are reports of frogs still with quivering dragonflies in their mouth which they cannot quite devour on account of the size.

Observations at the pond bring me from the idyll and from forgetting about death back into reality. Our civilization conceals death and hides it from society. To the ancient thinkers,[40] *memento mori* (remember death!) was a basic theme in daily life as well as in philosophy.

OLD AND NEW

Life and Death

In biology, death is almost as important as life. Without the trillionfold death of earlier living creatures, there would be no evolution of life, and we ourselves would not exist. The plundering murder of animals for the sake of food also has the side-effect (or is it the main reason?) of natural selection. Better chances of survival and a larger number of descendants determine the direction of development and the continuation of biological evolution. Animal species that could not adapt to an altered environment became extinct and thus made place for others. The biological benefits of death, however, make it no easier for us to bear. It remains a great catastrophe in life standing before each one of us. Death gives time the character of a limited duration, that of a lifetime bounded by birth and death.

Could nature work as well without death? In the course of the last half billion years, the Earth has been visited at least five times by global catastrophes. Somewhat less than the rotation period of the Sun in the Milky Way, 250 million years ago, there was a dramatic caesura in the biosphere, probably caused by volcanic activity in Siberia following large continental shifts. Massive streams of lava flowing into the sea, steaming water, emissions of sulfur dioxide, and aerosol of soot in the upper atmosphere permanently altered the climate. Only about 10 percent of all animal species survived, chiefly those with a mobile and predatory lifestyle. Even the insect kingdom was reduced by half. The altered climate so changed the plant and animal worlds that geologists today can still handily date their mineral samples in light of this event.

Other catastrophic climatic changes were caused by comets striking the Earth. Sixty-five million years ago, apparently induced by the impact of an eleven kilometer large meteorite in Chicxulub on the Yucatán Peninsula in Mexico, about half of all animal species, including the dinosaurs, became extinct within a few hundred thousand years. In the ensuing free living space, the quick-to-adapt mammals evolved in a sudden rush of development. They registered (perhaps precisely because of the preceding catastrophe) a great developmental leap forward. In the succeeding period of the tertiary, the human branch dissociated itself from the other mammals. The more dying there is, the faster the evolution.

Development through evolution proceeds quite differently from technical progress. A team of engineers, for instance, constructs a new telescope according to a detailed plan after painstaking calculations and exhausting discussions. But a female frog lays hundreds of eggs, each with a chemical blueprint for two eyes and a neural data reduction facility, more complicated and sophisticated than the latest telescope. Not only the design but even the automatic means of production for the eye is delivered in the form of macromolecular genes. One or two—perhaps none—of the eggs finally develops into a grown frog. For some insects, the chances of success are smaller than one in a million. A defective telescope is mended again and again. A wounded frog in our pond was, after a short time, eaten by the neighbor's cat, and another took its place. In its bleak severity, nature is limitlessly prodigal.

Nature is also lavish in cosmic dimensions. Only single stars or distant binaries can have planets, and only a small percentage of the stars in our galaxy are of type G as the Sun. It may be realistic to assume that about ten characteristics, each with a 10 percent probability of actualization, are necessary for a planet to be so earthlike that it could sustain life. Then only one in ten billion planets would have these preconditions and only one in ten galaxies would have such a planet. Even if these figures are possibly off by orders of magnitude, they indicate with what overpowering generosity the universe is furnished.

The extravagant fullness of life, but also the omnipresence of dying offered Jesus a parable for the creative vitality of his message, and was a starting point for his preaching:

A sower went out to sow. And as he sowed, some seed fell on the path, and the birds came and ate it up. Other seed fell on rocky ground, where it did not have much soil, and it sprang up quickly, since it had no depth of soil. And when the sun rose, it was scorched; and since it had no root, it withered away. Other seed fell among thorns, and the thorns grew up and choked it, and it yielded no grain. Other seed fell into good soil and brought forth grain, growing up and increasing and yielding thirty and sixty and a hundredfold.[41]

The new perception grows, according to Jesus, because God gives self-lessly. Although it only flourishes in good soil, the offer of a communicative relationship, the basis of this new vision, is disseminated as prodigiously and hazardously as the far-reaching, lavish dynamics of life itself.

How New Things Emerge

During a conference in Sicily, I lived in a hotel very close to an extensive expanse of ruins from an ancient Greek city. In my leisure time, I wandered through the ruins that had not been prepared for tourists, and attempted to imagine how the city might have looked in its heyday more than two thousand years ago. Only a few of the larger stones were left; most of the ruins lay scattered or in structureless piles of rubble. Earthquakes, enemies, builders, treasure hunters, and archeologists may all have had their effect. Remains of walls, roofs, temples, houses, and public buildings lay in utter confusion. Even the old streets could hardly be made out. The confusing jumble, and the loss of order and any sort of structure, were hardly surmountable.

The effect of the second law of thermodynamics was obviously apparent. This law states that entropy[42] remains the same or increases with time, implying above all that the information required for a complete description of a system must increase. The more the individual parts are mixed together and the greater the disorder, the greater the entropy and the more information is required to describe the whole. It would need generations of archeologists and the most modern means of support to put every stone back in its original place again and to approach restoration of the former order. The difference between ruin, which occurs "by itself," and the unimaginable effort to rebuild the old city at enormous expense shows once more the irreversible flow of time.

That the origin of the whole cosmos in the ancient views of the universe, in myths and creation narratives, was set at the beginning and even before the dawn of time does not come about by chance. How, in this world of decay, can order or even something new arise at all? This question is, at present, a fascinating topic in several different fields of inquiry. One example was already given in the description of the origin of stars. Stars form out of chance fluctuations in the interstellar gas. The development is, however, not accidental, although no external power exerts influence. The contraction strengthens by itself; once it has started, it goes faster and faster.

A self-strengthening process is *nonlinear*, for its growth increases during the course of the process. The interstellar medium is unstable; after a long initiatory period during which apparently nothing happens, the last phase of star formation moves along relatively quickly. Only the light of the far infrared and the millimeter waves can escape from within the contracting primeval nebula of young stars. If the million years of star formation could be shown in quick motion, one would see the contraction become faster and faster. At the end, the stars suddenly became visible, just as street lamps begin to light up in the evening. As a counterexample to the nonlinear process, the initially linear growth of the white dwarf of EM Cygni from chapter 1 may be mentioned. Matter from the companion rains steadily down upon it. Over a long period of time, the gain in matter has no influence on the white dwarf. Only when a considerable part of the companion has flowed over does its mass increase noticeably, and its attraction becomes greater. As a result, the rate of growth changes; the process becomes nonlinear. Finally the mass reaches its critical limit and the star explodes as a supernova.

Be it a star, a planet, a sunspot, or a tornado, the process of formation always occurs according to the same pattern: a system with free energy or with an external energy supply moves over a threshold of instability, begins to develop, and this alteration accelerates the process and strengthens accidental initial fluctuations by many orders of magnitude. In nonequilibrium, the chaotic initial condition develops into an ordered structure.

The process of self-strengthening does not proceed endlessly. After a certain time, secondary effects arise that work against the process. With the formation of stars, this is the heat of nuclear fusion in the new star. The nonlinear process is stopped, and one speaks of saturation. The self-organization[43] moves into a stationary flowing equilibrium. In this phase, still more energy is imported, set free, and expelled again as heat. This balance of input and output is only temporary and, after a particular period of apparent quiet, can suddenly be succeeded by further instability. The Sun will remain in its present, almost stable condition of saturation for 5.5 billion years longer until, after a spectacular red giant phase, it will move through its next contraction process to become a stable white dwarf.

Stellar winds and supernova explosions of old stars are triggers for new star formation. The old does not sink into nothing, but sometimes becomes part of the new. The chaos of ruin may provide the initial fluctuations, without which there would be no new structure. The point of departure of star formation is itself the result of earlier processes involving the self-organization of other stars and, originally, the formation of galaxies. In this manner a hierarchical order is established: clusters of galaxies enable the formation of galaxies,[44] and these moreover are the origin for stars, which produce the raw material for planets, upon which life can arise. On all levels, it concerns processes that are similar in the basic equations but that take place in various classes of size and in different temporal succession.

Novel Structures in the Universe

The atoms of the human body have a long history behind them. All stem from earlier processes that give rise to newness. The long chain leads from the formation of hydrogen nuclei, the protons, of clusters of galaxies and individual galaxies to early massive stars, which produced the elements heavier than oxygen, then on to the condensation of dust particles until the formation of planets. We bear within us the result of earlier cosmic events and the development of the universe. There would be no human beings without this chain of processes, which could be extended many times over through chemical, prebiotic, and finally biological evolution. The chain of earlier processes points to the historical interconnection of humanity with the whole cosmos. Yet if one pursues the stellar analogy, origin does not determine the final state. The fluctuation of the beginning does not fix the course of a self-organizing process. If a system has reached its attractor,[45] one can no longer reconstruct its formation in detail. The system has "forgotten" its origin. Therefore it is certainly incorrect to draw conclusions about the essence of being human from the course of human descent, be it through the animal kingdom or from a supernova. To be sure, a human being bears the old within, but is something quite different, something qualitatively new.

The example of star formation shows that the novel can *not* originate *everywhere*, but only in certain locations in the state of nonequilibrium. In particular, the new does not form arbitrarily, but *spontaneously*, as one knows well enough from the self-organizing low pressure systems of the Earth's atmosphere. A cyclone, originating suddenly over the ocean, can end a long period of balmy weather. It will never be possible to predict the weather for next year. Cyclones will certainly form, but it cannot be predicted when and where. It is the nonlinear and vacillating development—the so-called weak stability—of an enormous number of interacting air masses and, finally, of atmospheric molecules that prevents this.

Novel structures arise plentifully in the universe, but also in our daily surroundings. Naturally, we do not place the same subjective value on each new structure. Especially conspicuous are those points in time when new kinds of processes appeared and a new development started to evolve. Five essential take off points can be currently recognized, when fundamentally new possibilities were opened for cosmic development. In the first phase of the universe, the new came about through *breaks in symmetry* of elementary fields of force and particles. As the universe became transparent about a half million years after the Big Bang, the development changed to *self-organization of matter* thanks to the free energy of gravitation. Clusters of galaxies, galaxies, and stars formed as already described. After a few billion years, planets like Earth originated and, through their ideal conditions, enabled *chemical development* on the molecular level. This began with catalysis, the self-organization of chemical processes, and probably led to the origin of life after a few hundred million years. With biological reproduction, a myriad of new possibilities for development opened up, which kindled the *biological evolution* of the species. The chemical-biological evolution will be introduced and discussed in the following chapter.

After the simplest, single-celled creatures had originated early in Earth's history (Fig. 6), a further development period of almost three billion years was needed for multicellular organisms. After additional hundreds of millions of years and only in the course of the most recent

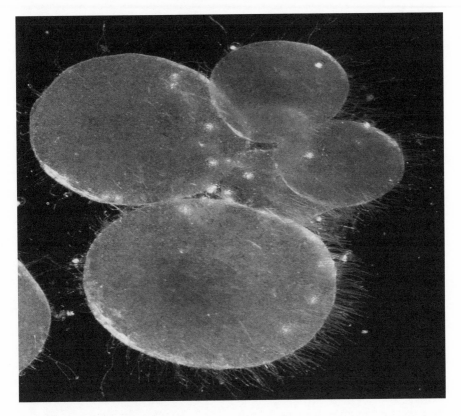

Figure 6: Blue-green algae measure less than a tenth of a millimeter in diameter. The predecessors of these unicellular organisms lived in marine and fresh water already 3.5 billion years ago. They are the oldest cells known (Photo: Dwight R. Kuhn).

million years, the development led finally to consciousness, a phenomenon difficult to grasp scientifically. It enabled a further dimension of development to take place, including the *cultural evolution* of human society. Cultural processes are also self-regulating and can strengthen themselves. One of these self-organizing cultural processes is science.

THE EVOLUTION OF LIVING BEINGS

The Life of Molecules

The step from single atoms to the complexity of the simplest living creatures is unimaginably large and still obscure in many regards. In the second half of the twentieth century, several partial processes have been explained so that the hypothesis of life's origin from inanimate matter has been strengthened. Among scientists, the opinion is widespread that self-organizing processes must have played a decisive role in this breakthrough.

In order to do justice to the complexity of life, which surpasses the complexity of all manmade machines by many orders of magnitude, we must place ourselves before the enormous difficulties that face biochemical research. One instance is demonstrated by the molecule of deoxyribonucleic acid (DNA), the hereditary substance of all living beings. It is contained also in the simplest virus and is made up of over 10,000 small molecular building blocks, the nucleotides. Most of the time, only four of their kind are present. Their disposition in the DNA molecule constitutes the totality of hereditary information. Is it conceivable that the correct arrangement of nucleotides came about purely by accident? Let us assume for a moment that all of the ca. 10^{75} carbon atoms in the observable universe banded together into nucleotides, which were newly grouped every millionth of a second in sequences of ten thousand respectively. The probability that the correct succession of nucleotides for a single DNA molecule had formed purely by chance just once since the origin of the universe, would be one in 10^{5900}. The well-known astrophysicist Fred Hoyle has remarked that this is as improbable as the accidental construction of a jumbo jet out of its single components in a junkyard, over which a whirlwind sweeps. This improbability is actually so large that it is equivalent to exclusion. It is still much greater in more complex creatures and in humans. Some scientists have capitulated before this difficulty and regard the origin of life as inexplicable.

Before science declares itself incapable of establishing the origin of life, the prerequisites for the probability calculation must be reexamined. It is not only improbable, but chemically unimaginable, that ten thousand nucleotides spontaneously unite into a single molecule. Chemical reactions of this sort proceed over many intermediate steps, and this process demands a totally different calculation. From step to step, the molecules become larger and more varied, and the rule according to which the chemical reactions take place is not pure chance.

In the following, five phases of development through which life could have arisen will be described. Each one comprises many chemical reactions and steps. The five phases are only a schematic synopsis of the latest state of biochemical findings and ignorance.

In the first phase, atoms and molecules actually meet by chance through collisions and unite in small organic molecules. Only in this phase does chance operate thus. Since, however, the molecules were constructed out of only a few atoms, the chance to form was not prohibitive. In a famous experiment in 1952, S. Miller and H. Urey simulated the primeval atmosphere of Earth in a laboratory. For one week, they sent electric discharges through a mixture of various gases assumed to exist in the primeval atmosphere, including methane, ammonia, and water vapor, but not oxygen. They illuminated the mixture with intense ultraviolet radiation. Already in the first experiment, four different *amino acids* were formed. They are the basis for proteins and enzymes such as fatty acids and urea, which are vital to life. Through variations in the chemical composition and through other stimuli such as heat pulses or shock waves, Miller and Urey could finally synthesize the twenty most important amino acids. Amino acids are molecules composed of ten to twenty-five hydrogen, carbon, oxygen, and nitrogen atoms. Later experiments have also yielded some similarly constructed *nucleotides*, the building blocks of nucleic acids.

The second phase presumably took place in water, where the molecules dissolved that were formed in the first phase. Not only did single atoms accumulate, but small molecules united into larger ones. In addition to chance collisions, electromagnetic attraction became more important and finally determined the reaction rates. One of many possible products that formed then in this primeval soup was *pantetheine*. This was convincingly confirmed in suitable experiments. Pantetheine is particularly interesting since it is a part of the important biological molecule coenzyme A, upon which many enzymes and other biochemical substances are based.

In the third step, these molecules combined to produce *polymers*. This group of threadlike macromolecules wrapped like a net or a ball of yarn includes simple nucleic acids and proteins. Promising experiments are being conducted with the goal of constructing these large biochemical molecules on the surfaces of small solid particles in watery solutions. Dozens of nucleotides unite to form long chains of polymers on suspended clay minerals. It is within the realm of possibility that in such suspensions, enzymes have developed. They are special proteins that function like catalysts and accelerate a chemical reaction without being used up in the process. Most relevant biochemical reactions are based on enzymes. Among the enzymes vital to life are also those with auto-catalytic characteristics, through which a compound can reproduce itself. In an auto-catalytic process, the reaction partners become more numerous, so the process occurs more often and accelerates the multiplication. The mathematical equations that describe auto-catalytic processes are, in part, identical with those of star formation. These prebiotic developments are also self-organizing processes.

Up until this point, chemistry must have proceeded in relatively unregulated fashion. In the fourth step, a new kind of development began, in which chemical reactions were limited to small zones and controlled through nonlinearity and saturation. The Russian biochemists V. Fok and A. Oparin have shown that so-called micro-drops could form with a membranelike covering. The *membrane* divides the protocells from the outside world and is the place where catalytic reactions run their course and make possible the targeted exchange between the internal and the external.

The fifth phase, in which these cell-like formations began to multiply, still remains largely incomprehensible. It is certain that DNA molecules developed only during this step and took over their role as central regulatory mechanism and information carrier of the *cell*. DNA has the form of a doubly wound spiral and is arranged in humans in about 100,000 logical blocks, the genes. A single gene is composed of about a thousand simple building blocks, the aforementioned nucleotides. The long path from nucleotides to DNA had certainly led over many simpler nucleic acids. An important intermediary step was perhaps the ribonucleic acid (RNA). It consists of nucleotides similar to DNA, except that it normally does not form double-stranded spirals, but single-roped chains. RNA molecules are catalytically active and also play an important role today, in that they read the genetic code of DNA and, according to this instruction, produce cell-specific proteins. It is possible that the fifth phase itself consisted out of several, still unknown phases. It was surely the largest step that the chemical development had mastered.

It is certainly true that knowledge about the origin of life is still sketchy and full of gaps. These, however, are not so severe that one must regard the appearance of this novel structure of the universe as wholly inexplicable in scientific terms. Present knowledge can already interpret some of the puzzling qualities of life on Earth. The striking chemical uniformity of all life follows naturally from the hypothesis of a common origin of life in the primeval soup of our Earth's first billion years. The enormous variety of the macromolecules of all living creatures, necessary for vital metabolism and as genetic material, is formed from the same few ingredients: twenty amino acids and five nucleotides. With a little imagination, one could think up completely different possibilities of organic chemistry. The simplicity of the chemical means from which life ensues points to a common source, or a common formal origin of all life. During a long evolution, living beings have adjusted again and again to the changeable environment and have spread out over the whole Earth: bacteria are found in the depths of the sea, nine thousand meters below the surface, and from the highest layers of the atmosphere to rocks amid steaming hot springs and sulfurous dampness.

This adaptability of life should not lead to the assumption that life could arise under almost arbitrary conditions. The results of biochemistry make clear that, given the oxygen present in the *current* atmosphere of Earth, life can no longer originate from inorganic material. The intensity of the ultraviolet radiation from the Sun, the frequency of electric discharges, impacting meteorites, as well as the methane and ammonia content of the air have also decreased to the point that, were all life to be extinguished, Earth could never again reach the primeval condition in which life can form.

Let us summarize. Chemical reactions do not follow simple chance processes of single atoms. Catalytic and auto-catalytic processes can multiply a rare substance and supply the material that initiates a succeeding reaction. They shorten the length of development by many orders of magnitude. The initially mentioned improbability certainly does not do justice to biochemical life processes. *Life has not arisen by chance, but by self-organization.* Self-amplifying processes appear sporadically and locally, and cause development to become a nonlinear phenomenon, whose probability and efficiency cannot yet be reliably calculated. Even when there is still no unique and closed theory of the origin of life—and perhaps there never will be one—a scenario can be sketched by which life could have arisen in accord with these processes. The requirements for such may be difficult to fulfill, but if the preconditions are present, simple, one-celled living creatures could arise within a few hundred million years. In this way, it is understandable why life in the form of unicellular microorganisms came into being on Earth fewer than 800 million years after the formation of the solar system—that is, just about at the earliest imaginable period of time.

Evolution of the Theory of Evolution

The further development of living beings was also more varied and complicated than one had thought earlier. The evolution of the species did not run as uniformly as Charles Darwin had postulated in the nineteenth century. When he was a doctoral student, the paleontologist Niles Eldredge searched for years for petrified trilobites in order to ascertain how they had changed in the course of Earth's history. They resembled today's woodlouse but were ten times as large. Soon after they first appeared, 570 million years ago, they spread over the whole Earth and developed into thousands of species. During the Paleozoic Era, a particular subgroup of these extinct animals was to be widely found in the ocean that covered the present American continent. Eldredge excavated layer after layer. Over a period of many millions of years, the trilobites did not reveal the slightest alteration. Then, however, in a certain layer, and without any transition, the young researcher discovered a change in the number of eye lenses.

It was only years later that Eldredge found the solution to the mystery in a deposit on the edge of the extended habitat of these trilobites. In that peripheral territory, where the fight for survival was probably especially hard and full of losses, there were transitional forms of trilobite eyes. Here, in a small space and relatively quickly, Eldredge found acted out what Darwin alleged to be the survival of the fittest. In a geographically isolated splinter group fighting for survival, mutated genes bear greater weight. Trilobites with the new kind of eye grew better and multiplied faster in face of the challenge of the local environment. In the end, they not only dominated their place of origin but also spread and suppressed the old kind of trilobite in other regions. In geological terms, this adaptation apparently happened overnight.

A spatial aspect is superimposed on the temporal aspect of evolution. As a result of migration, different species meet. Competition takes place also on the level of species—that is, not only among individuals of the same species, as Darwin postulated. Different species compete for the same living space. The fittest suppresses others and survives.

The development of new biological forms demonstrates how creativity itself develops. Biological evolution is also subject to evolution. It is with good reason that biologists resist the tendency to subsume biological evolution within the mathematical equations and terms of physics. Nevertheless, it is helpful to consider what physics and biology hold in common as regards evolution.

Biological species are stable over thousands of years, although environmental influences such as cosmic radiation constantly cause genetic mutations. This property corresponds to the fluctuation of a physical system in indifferent equilibrium. An example of this type of equilibrium is a cube on a horizontal surface. The cube is pelted with small projectiles from all directions and slides with a jagged, random motion. If one gives the surface a very weak gradient, the cube is no longer in equilibrium, and its zigzag course tends in the direction of the slope. Something similar happens when a biological species is placed in a changing environment so that individuals with certain qualities survive and reproduce better. The gene pool, the totality of genes of all living individuals of the species, changes systematically. Finally a new species arises. The evolutionary potential corresponds to the slope and the available energy of the cube. Evolutionary pressure may operate only within a limited area, as with the trilobites, and it can change direction as time goes on. That is the case with climatic changes, as when a thick jungle turns into an open savanna. Depending on the particular environmental conditions, either small, flexible living beings or large, strong creatures may be preferred.

Today, our technical civilization alters the evolutionary slope of the human development so quickly that the direction of evolution is not clear. Technical and medicinal intervention enable more and more human beings to survive and procreate. One could theorize that technical civilization itself, or culture in general, has become the ground of human evolution, and that there exist no more gradients for biological development in the human species.

Since the time of Eldredge's discoveries, further proofs have been found that the continuing development of certain species moves very slowly. Striking mutants are usually not able to live. But every creature differs in minor ways from every other (for instance, in its specific proteins), even if it looks very similar externally. These small changes apparently affect evolution very little or not at all. Small alterations play an important role only when the fight for survival is hard. Under pressure of adversity, evolution proceeds quickly. In the interglacial period before the last ice age, the Neanderthals occupied an ecological niche that had arisen in the ice-free part of Europe. During the following climatic catastrophe, they were superseded by our ancestral Homo sapiens, who stood up better to the stress of survival during the Ice Age. With the retreating glaciers, our species propagated in a short time over the whole Earth—to Europe, Australia, and America.

One may conjecture that mutations of living beings are nature's sport. But then selection in the fight for survival is a merciless suffering. Biological progress is bought with tears. Worse still, one realizes that suffering is no guarantee of higher development. Often death seems to be a setback, or the brutal end of a development.

The Role of Death

The red flour beetle, *Tribolium castaneum*, is today a widespread and feared storeroom pest, found everywhere on Earth. It can be fought with the insecticide Malathion, among others. A few years ago, investigators were surprised to discover that this poison suddenly lost its potency in certain locales, where the beetle multiplied without hindrance. The Canadian biologist Robert Dunbrack wanted to get to the bottom of this phenomenon and took advantage of the beetle's high procreation rate for the following experiment. He divided red flour beetles evenly into two containers. Both groups were regularly fed, but with a sparse ration for the number of beetles so that they faced the pressure of competition.

The food of both groups contained a small dose of Malathion—not deadly, but unhealthy for the beetles. In the first container, Dunbrack took out the freshly hatched offspring and replaced them with beetles from a reserve group that had never been exposed to Malathion. Through this method, he prevented every adaptation and development. In the second container, he allowed evolution to run its course.

At first, the population that had its development blocked multiplied better because the new beetles were already capable of procreating. But the original contingent was weakened by the poison, and the fresh beetles ate the food of the old ones so that they had fewer offspring. The total number of beetles in the first container subsequently decreased. Finally, the developmentally hindered population became extinct. The same thing happened when Dunbrack replaced every offspring with three new beetles.

What happened in the evolving group was different: at first it looked very critical for them. The weakened red flour beetles had few offspring, from which only a small number survived. In a series of experiments, the number of subjects sank to a fiftieth of their original number. After five generations, the situation reversed itself dramatically. There were, apparently, always beetles for whom the Malathion caused less trouble than for the others. A characteristic of their genetic material, developed by chance, made them somewhat better able to resist the poison. The beetles that adapted better to the insecticide survived, became more resistant with every generation, and also competed successfully with the older generations in the pursuit of nourishment. Their number finally exceeded the initial numbers and continued to rise until the experiment was concluded.

This experiment shows dramatically how an animal species can persist by selective adaptation in a sequence of generations. *Through the death of individuals, the species survives when conditions for life change.*

A particular species of living beings, more exactly the total set of its genes, develops similarly to a self-organizing physical system. For physical structures to originate, the accumulating and disturbing heat energy must be able to flow away so that the process can proceed further. The flowing equilibrium of star formation, and with it the order, would again disintegrate without the discharge of contraction heat through radiation. In biological evolution, every animal species corresponds to a system in flowing equilibrium. The heat drain of a physical system corresponds to the death of the individual in biological development. Thanks to this death, species do not remain fixed but can adapt themselves in some measure to an altered environment. Life requirements alter continually in the wake of climatic changes, variations in the chemical composition of air and water, food supply, global catastrophes, and as new competition appears and enemies become extinct. Without death, there would be no adaptive selection. It has enabled higher forms of life, reaching to humanity, to develop.

Some readers may be irritated to find how lightly death is discussed in science, even though it is a heavy burden in the life of individual human beings. Faithful to its methods, science screens out the subjective side of suffering and death. In this case, however, the required objectivity seems difficult to achieve. The thinking subject bristles when asked to consider death with actual indifference and finds it difficult to contemplate mortality scientifically. It is hard for the conscious mind to externalize and objectify its own decease as though it would not be personally affected. To classify one's own death as a small step in the development of the universe is no consolation in view of the defects and dead ends in evolution. Even if this step seemed scientifically to signify progress, it would still have no significance unless evolution as a whole had a meaning. Such an affirmation, however, is not possible on the objective, causal language level of science.

Science does not offer a relationship of human existence to death, neither to one's own passing nor to that of another living creature. Causal explanations offer no personal connection; the separation of subject and object fails in this regard. Personal and scientific perceptions are completely different. The next section will examine death from the standpoint of creation. We shall make a big leap, then, to find ourselves on the level of religious language that inquires into the motives of God's activity.

THE NEXUS OF DEATH

The notion that in this world, in space and time, something new can actually come about, as has entered our field of view in astrophysics—and earlier in biology and geology—is likewise essential to Christianity. According to Judeo-Christian understanding, the world develops. Lasting changes occur, and in the future that will arise what has never been before. Understood as sacred history, time marches forth from the patriarchs, through Jesus, into an open future—and, indeed, to a definitive end. The development is not cyclical. Time does not repeat itself, and God's action lets the old fall away and the new arise.

Within Christian tradition, one finds different ideas about how the new originates. One of these envisions the new arising out of nothingness. This view has biblical (2 Maccabees 7:28) as well as Neo-Platonic roots. In 400 A.D., Augustine connected these ideas to a doctrine that left its stamp on Western culture to modern times and is widespread even today. It has also been evoked in the first part of this book, where the present was perceived from the standpoint of new time approaching us as if created out of nothing. Here, though, I would like to emphasize the other, older tradition, according to which the new does not arise out of nothing but is formed from what is already available, from decay and the old. In this view, the new is in fact already here—one must only notice it in the present. The Old Testament delivers an instructive example of how to expect this newness. Jerusalem was conquered and demolished in the year 587 B.C. by Nebuchadnezzar and the people deported to Babylon. The kingdom of the House of David was wiped out, the temple was destroyed, and the culture and religion of the Israelites were in decay. The prophet, who was also carried off, indicates hope to his people with the words: "Thus says the Lord: . . . I am about to do a new thing; now it springs forth, do you not perceive it?" (Isaiah 43:16, 19 NSRV). This affirmation does not suppose that all will again be as it was before. Rather, this perception of time contains a realism that takes the here and now seriously and trusts in a *new* future. It will not be like the past; the prophet faces up to the irreversibility of time.

Similarities between the scientific and religious perceptions of time marching irreversibly along are not accidental—modern science did originate and grow in Christian Europe. Although the Judeo-Christian conception of time did not flow into the sciences in a straight line, it nonetheless created the prerequisites for comprehending the world not as a given, but as developing.

The defining experience of Christian faith is the resurrection. It was for those involved not simply one miracle among many, but an experience that irreversibly changed their world. In the light of Easter, the first Christians comprehended the world in a new way. In Easter, they found a pattern that affords understanding of how God acts in other contexts as well. In this form and in this perspective, the resurrected Christ was still present; he was already in the far-distant past, even before the created universe, and he will also be in the future. Easter is the central creation story of Christianity and shows by example what is meant by creation in the here and now. This less familiar notion of newness emerging from current reality deserves further comment.

Two Levels of Resurrection

On the level of objectifying language and causal explanations, we may assume that the execution of the well-known miracle worker Jesus of Nazareth on the day before the beginning of the feast of the passover in the year 31 A.D. is historic. It was recorded in Roman and Jewish historic writings opposed to Christianity. With few exceptions, the inhabitants of Jerusalem surely celebrated their holiday as always, despite the Gospels' report of an empty grave. Outside observers have left us no hint of objective phenomena that are not physically and medically explainable. For the empty grave, there was even a causal explanation that the evangelist Matthew did not accept but passed on: theft of the corpse. The actual event remained obscure; thunder and earthquakes were probably only later connected with it. Externally, the Easter happening was so unspectacular that the early Christians attested: "He was in the world . . . yet the world did not know him" (John 1:10). In any event, an obvious *consequence* of Easter was soon visible also for the Pharisees and the Romans: the extraordinarily dynamic community of Christians in Jerusalem. Its formation may be sociologically understandable in retrospect, but was hardly to be predicted. It was certainly not planned. For the world at that time, it was something new that came about spontaneously.

The closer people were involved in the event, however, the more they were touched. The resurrected Jesus, a new world, appeared to them on this Earth. I can imagine that they did not respond indifferently or objectively to this phenomenon. Instead, they reacted personally and emotionally, as is characteristic of religious perceptions. Interestingly, one reads in 1 Corinthians 15:7-9 that the resurrected Jesus appeared not only to the disciples and former followers but also to an admitted opponent, the later Paul. Those involved could only grasp these unprecedented experiences by developing new religious concepts. They perceived, expressed, and explained the events on the level of participatory faith.

Different Conceptions of God

The first Christians understood the resurrection neither as a divine correction of a human judicial murder nor as the happy ending of a tragic accident, but much more as the onset of a new era.[46] They confronted not a simple repetition of the old but a new, future form of life that nevertheless encompassed the old. It was reported that the new body of the risen Christ still bore the wounds of the crucifixion (John 20:25). Jesus' death and the catastrophe of Good Friday are constantly portrayed as real in the Gospels. The new took the first Christians so much by surprise that they could only explain it as a spontaneous act of creation by God, from whom they knew by their tradition that "he will be, who he will be" (Exodus 3:14).

The narration of Good Friday and Easter contains the curious thought that God participates in suffering in this world. Even if a man is tortured to death in the most horrible manner, God is there. Jesus, hanging on the cross, attests to that in gripping fashion with the words:

"My God, my God, why have you forsaken me?" (Matthew 27:46; Psalm 22:2). With these words Jesus does not express God's abandonment, as a superficial reading might suggest, but quotes the beginning of a psalm that moves from lament to praise. The conclusion of the psalm known by every pious Jew prophesies that coming generations would still praise God for participating justice. In modern Christian theology, the image persists of God dying on the cross.[47] Obviously, God is here introduced not as an impersonal power, who from a great distance and beyond all suffering has in mind only the great goal of evolution. Rather, God's nearness, even in suffering and dying, is a key element of Jesus' message.[48] The symbol of the cross in the early church made it clear that Good Friday and Easter form a whole, and that affliction is not effaced in the midst of Easter jubilation and hope for life beyond death.

If in previous chapters our discussion largely concerned a sovereignly acting creator God, a completely different idea of God now faces us in Jesus' death on the cross. From the standpoint of modern science, that understanding of a God who thunders down with fire and lightning or arbitrarily rules the world as absolute monarch has certainly outlived its usefulness. The new often arises inconspicuously and is then as vulnerable as a newborn child. In the "new song of praise" we tried to see how the scientifically explainable world can be perceived on the language level of Christian faith as a creation. In this view, the universe exists only through God's free will, even if this will remains subtly in the background and is not directly provable. God's omnipotence remains uncontested. What we confront on Good Friday is, on the contrary, powerlessness and lowliness. The task of reconciling these two divergent conceptions of God has occupied Christians for two thousand years. Undoubtedly, the contradictions cannot be wholly eliminated. Yet, as we have seen, objectively perceived reality in science is also full of contradictions and tensions. How could it be any different with God?[49]

Sympathetic Faith

Both levels of language—objective and participatory, relating respectively to scientific-historic reason and to faith—remain as distinct as they were two thousand years ago. Paul had to experience that in Athens: "When they heard of resurrection of the dead, some scoffed; but others said, 'We will hear you again about this' " (Acts 17:32). Since the historical facts concerning Easter cannot be reconstructed and therefore the objectively perceptible event remains speculative, the two levels stay disjunct today. The resurrection remains for us, as previously for the citizens of Athens, an unsettling experience linked to the participatory perception of a small group on the edge of the Roman Empire. It is arresting to observe what dynamic developed from this experience and how its tidings spread over the entire Roman Empire within a generation, and later throughout the whole world. The reason for this resonance in a time so rich in miracles was not the singularity of the Good Friday/Easter event, but rather its exemplary nature: such an occurrence allows for the hope that in other crises something similar will happen.

Good Friday/Easter became for Christians a new pattern for life, a paradigm with which they discovered the world anew. The old basic facts of life confronted them as they always had, and the same needs plagued them, but they perceived therein a new, deeper dimension. Even if the present is destroyed and no fortunate solution appears possible, all is not yet lost. God can create something completely new that far exceeds the boldest expectations. This principle holds also for one's own life, in which death must be confronted, as well as for catastrophes that affect all humankind. The expectation may not be fulfilled, at least not in the manner one wishes. For the new is no automaton, which would turn God's free act into a causal event. The future remains open and subject to risk. Christians nevertheless gather from the Good Friday/Easter experience a hope that death will not be the last word, just as Good Friday was not the endpoint it first appeared.

The core of the Easter story is a tale told not only to its original audience, but also to people of today, who thereby gain awareness of a further dimension of reality in the development of the universe, of Earth, and of life. Christians see the world with new eyes, trusting in God's suffering and acting on Good Friday and Easter. In the face of suffering associated with evolution and death, a human being imbued with this faith can perceive God's sympathetic participation on Good Friday. Something analogous to the creative act of Easter strikes us in the unexpected, overwhelming newness of spontaneously emerging novel structures. The new and the decaying, both birth and death, become transparent so as to disclose the divine. This transparency reveals no new causal explanations or scientific facts. Rather, those who perceive in this way are placed into a new and personal relationship to the world.

Theologians could rightfully object that we have until now considered only one aspect of the paschal events. This, however, is not the place for complete theological explications. My primary intent is rather to make understandable for our time what has been seen as exemplary about these events over the past two thousand years. Although much about them has become incomprehensible or obsolete, a father today may still view the birth of his child as a wonder comparable to Easter. Furthermore, the newness of Easter can also be compared to scientific models of formation. Scientific facts are thus understood as comparable to the contents of belief on the religious level. The central creation story of Christianity, that of Good Friday and Easter, then sheds a different light on the most dismal chapters of evolution. Biology and faith encounter one another.

It must finally be emphasized that the Good Friday/Easter scheme is not a usual paradigm which, like a simple model, elucidates a complicated state of affairs. Rather, the original event has been a rich source of inspiration and multilayered interpretation for the past two millennia. Eventually we shall consider further its significance for Christian hope. The view of Easter as a creative act of God requires participation and is, in the end, only to be conceived of as a revelation. Easter does not invite us to comprehension in the scientific or historical sense, but rather to participation. The early Christians celebrated this discovery with a feast on the first day of every week, an actual embodiment of participation.

THESIS

T he universe has a fascinating history. It is a tale of order forming out of chaos, from the startling appearance of newness as a revolutionary structuring of the already existent. The new does not arise out of nothingness, but out of existing material whose structure is in decay. On another level of perception requiring participation, something in the first instance enigmatic and overwhelmingly new is experienced in the Easter event, which appeared for the original disciples amid a broken world.

Good Friday and Easter revolutionize the traditional conception of God. God is recognized now as one who takes part in the suffering of decay and, at the same time, as one who creates new form and order. Such events are here understood as exemplary and as a pattern in the light of which the universe's past and future development becomes a story of creation. The paschal events thus become the keystone of Christianity's interpretation of the universe. If one perceives scientifically discernible development through the optics of Good Friday and Easter, it becomes creation. The universe gains a new dimension: hope.

This thesis is not provable in the way a mathematical proposition would be. Illustrations of the universe's development from its beginning to the dawn of human consciousness do not inevitably call up religious questions or answers. The reality that appears through science can, however, serve as a metaphor that makes perceptions intelligible on a wholly different level. On that other level of perception, personal participation and faith are essential. The final section of this book should make this thesis clear and show by way of application how hope may emerge in the view of future developments.

Part 4

THE

FUTURE

SENSATIONS OF THE FUTURE

While reading a long-term study of new telescopes in space, I recently came upon the year 2030. I tried to imagine how our world will look then. As a point of departure, I took contemporary astronomy and currently visible trends. First I considered which astronomical projects would be concluded, which problems solved, and which tasks accomplished. How could the economy develop that would have to bear the costs of research in the year 2030? What would be the most favorable development, as predicted from current tendencies? How could I contribute to this progress and what effort would prove most worthwhile? These new projects and goals stirred my fantasy. As I concentrated my thought deliberately on the best possible future, I felt a physical change within myself. My body relaxed, my breathing was deep and restful, and I felt security and cheerful expectation. That mood lasted only so long, until I began to reflect on negative prospects for the future. What problems could appear? What hopes could still be entertained if certain symptoms of decay in society became stronger? What catastrophic events such as plagues, political upheavals, wars, and economic collapse could appear in the coming decades? And, finally, what would I have to confront personally on the level of sickness, pain, or death? In seconds, not only did my psychological feelings change, but I also felt a bodily alteration. Apparently at this moment, a molecular message was directed into the blood which changed the character of my breathing, circulation, and musculature. Since then, I have repeated this experiment a few times; when I give it full concentration, it always produces the same response.

The future unleashes all sorts of feelings within us. Joyful anticipation of something other or new can give wings to our work. A fascinating goal may be regenerative, creating an impetus that feeds back on itself. In contrast, anxiety and thoughts of future misfortune can be disabling. In recent years, news about unfamiliar agents of illness has at times spread waves of anxiety through the general populace. Although such maladies have claimed less than one percent of the deaths recorded annually from traffic fatalities, we are apt to imagine them spreading uncontrollably to the point of soon carrying off half of humankind. Yet both feelings about the future, enthusiasm and anxiety, have less to do with the future itself than with the image we ourselves create of it.

From the point of view of developmental biology, one may surmise that certain feelings improve the survival chances of human beings and that feelings have thus been a criterion for selection in our species. This response stands in contrast to the experience of emotions that impair our ability to act rationally when the future weighs heavily upon us. Nevertheless, people who suffer a brain injury and become disturbed in their world of feelings, often find it difficult to make rational choices and to live out the results of their decisions.[50] Feelings can actually replace missing information and logic. Moreover, there are feelings about the future that compel us to apply in our lives solutions we rationally know to be correct. The intellect alone is not sufficient to survive in our society.

Through feelings, but also through our expectations, plans, and goals, the future is already to be found in the present. I am influenced not only by my past, but also by my sense of the future. What awaits a person claims a commanding place in one's heart and head and, though still far away, is not to be discounted. It is better to acknowledge these feelings than to suppress them, because otherwise they may show up unexpectedly in exaggerated or destructive ways. The best survival strategy in regards to the future is a balanced relationship between feeling and intellect.

In this last section, I shall consider in more detail how the question of the future is shaped by perceptions grounded in scientific findings, as well as by those in which the subject participates.

THE FUTURE IS OPEN

We have noticed previously that the past history of the universe has led repeatedly to surprising, novel structures and unexpected new dimensions. This finding leads us to conclude that cosmic development is open-ended. How is this possible, as in fact it runs its course according to scientific laws? An open future would mean that what lies ahead is not yet determined and will be decided only later. Whether this openness is intrinsic or follows necessarily from the ever-limited accuracy of measurement would make no difference in practice. That the ongoing history of humankind has an open future in the face of human freedom is easier to accept than the open future of the universe. Freedom, after all, is an anthropological term, not a subject of physics. When openness is attributed to matter, suspicions of anthropological projection are aroused. Isn't a physical object—an electron, for example—more aptly described in opposite terms of compulsion? According to these rigid laws, causality can be mathematically represented in physics through exact differential equations and symmetries. Such equations are strictly deterministic: the initial conditions predetermine the future. In the twentieth century, though, this mechanical view of the world was pierced and enlarged through two new concepts in physics. With quantum mechanics *chance* entered the picture, and with nonlinear dynamics came *chaos*. In the new view of the universe, the future is therefore undetermined within a certain framework. How might we describe the material basis of this openness?

Chance Is Part of Physics

As previously explained, quantum mechanical chance occurs in measurement. The observer finds the electron in an accidental location. Before the measurement, the location of the electron is uncertain and only known as a probability. After measuring, one may know its location exactly but the momentum—velocity times mass—is not known. Quantum mechanics relates the uncertainties in location and momentum: its product must be greater than Planck's constant. Uncertainty allows for the dual nature of matter, in that particles are also waves. One may envision the electron as a cloudlike distribution in space. If this probability distribution now strikes the fluorescent screen of a detector, a flash goes off in a certain location. The electron is thus manifested as a particle in this place. The location in question cannot be calculated in advance through a scientific law and can only be described through a probability. According to the Copenhagen interpretation of quantum mechanics, the reason for this is that the particle has first taken shape in the moment of measurement. Chance is therefore part of physical reality.

Not surprisingly, this new concept of chance did not win ready acceptance in view of the fundamental postulate of physics—causality. Albert Einstein, in particular, expressed the suspicion that chance is only apparent because the parameters engendering it are not yet known to us. It took more than half a century until experiments[51] corroborated that chance was really involved and cannot be replaced by a causal explanation.

In physics, the term "chance" does not mean arbitrariness. The "law of the large number" operates also in the realm of quantum mechanical chance. One can easily test this law with a die. With one throw of the die, the result between 1 and 6 is equally probable. Now we throw the die a thousand times and add up the numbers. The result will, with great probability, equal about 3500, a thousand times the mean value. In ninety percent of the cases, one receives a value of plus or minus 90 of the mean value. The estimate of 3500 is then accurate within 2.5 percent. Naturally, the minimal sum of 1000 is also possible, if only 1's are thrown. Yet this case happens on the average only once in 10^{778} tries and can practically be excluded, considering that only $3.8 \cdot 10^{17}$ seconds have passed since the beginning of the universe. With 100,000 throws of the die, the mean value yields an estimate which involves an error margin of less than

0.25 percent. The experiment of the die thus shows how chance can lose its randomness with an increasing number of trials.

Much of modern electronics rests upon the laws of chance. Whether, for example, a single electron passes through a tunnel diode is pure chance. In this process, a particle penetrates a potential barrier, which would permit no infringement according to strict energy conservation. The potential is like an incline toward which a ball rolls. If the ball lacks velocity to surmount the obstacle, it rolls a distance up the incline and then back. In quantum mechanics, the picture is different. Most of the particles will be similarly reflected, of course. Yet a certain percentage of them will appear on the opposite side because their energy and location are uncertain. Whether a certain electron will tunnel through the potential is not predictable. If many attempts can be made, however, one can predict how many particles will pass through within a very small margin of error, as by the throwing of dice. Modern computers contain tunnel diodes, which are based upon this chance process and deliver reliable results. Chance within the world of quantum becomes a calculable law in the macroscopic world.

However, if only a single quantum event occurs—for example, the impact of a cosmic high-energy particle into a gene—its location is accidental in the truest sense of the word and has no casual explanation.

A few words on the subject of "chance and God" may be necessary at this juncture. Too often in the past, quantum mechanical chance has been equated with a divine will. However, the biblical narratives always cite a particular reason for the intervention of God, for instance, God's compassion or rancor against a nation or a single individual. This activity is understood as providential, not as blind chance. Jewish and Christian thinkers consciously distinguished God's historic interventions from the fatalism envisioned in the ancient world. In their view, neither the fates nor blind chance determined the course of events, but rather a God of purposeful design. On the *religious level of discourse*, God could thus be denoted as the reason why chance is possible at all. Both law *and* chance reflect God's creative activity; through both of these, our world maintains itself and develops. Personally, I can more readily associate God with the creation of time than with the operations of chance. Through its progressive, irreversible character, time brings reality out of the world of quantum. Time is central in this truly creative act and makes chance happen.

Chaos Limits Our Knowledge

In the new worldview of science, particularly in astrophysics, time is the center point. Thus it is not surprising that physics today conceives of chaos in terms of a *process*. In this context, "chaos" does not signify what is designated in the Old Testament and Greek cosmologies as a mythic primeval condition or substance from which the world is formed into an ordered cosmos either through the activity of a creator or by itself. Closer to this original meaning, though, is an older use of the word "chaos" in physics to signify the thermal motion of molecules or density fluctuations in gases.[52] This older concept of chaos denotes the muddle of immeasurably numerous particles which, on the microscopic level, move in constantly varying interactions and collisions. Out of such chaotic motion, order can arise by self-organization.

In present-day terms, *a process of physics is termed "chaotic" if its long-term course is not predictable*. As often in the past, a word originating from an entirely different context becomes a label for an exactly defined scientific phenomenon. This new concept of physics nevertheless deserves general attention. The word "chaos" contains a fresh understanding, which reflects something of a revolution in the way physicists think about physics in the second half of the twentieth century.

Processes in physics are normally represented with equations, describing the behavior of a system in time. One terms such behavior *deterministic*. If the current location and the velocity are known, the trajectory can be calculated for the whole of the future and the past. These equations can be simple, as with the orbit of a single planet around the Sun. The further into the future or past one calculates, the more imprecision accumulates from small defects in the original values. For instance, an inexact velocity obviously leads to an ever-increasing error in position. This inaccuracy increases linearly over time: in double the time, it is twice as large.

Surprisingly this linear increase in uncertainty no longer holds if many planets encircle the Sun and interact with each other. Small errors do not increase linearly with time but in nonlinear fashion, mostly exponentially. Thus, the error in prediction grows ever faster the longer the time. After a few exponential growth-times, the errors grow so large that one cannot predict where in its orbit a planet will be. Such behavior is termed *deterministically chaotic*. The mathematical reason lies in the greater number of equations and the coupling of the parameters. The orbits of such a system diverge strongly. For instance, two interplanetary space probes with slightly different velocities in the immediate vicinity of one another will be in quite different locations in the solar system after a sufficient length of time.

Even the orbit of the Earth around the Sun, regarded formerly as a model example of an eternal motion, is chaotic. If the Earth's current position is exactly known to 15 centimeters, one cannot calculate where it will find itself in its annual orbit around the Sun in 120 million years. Small disturbances through the other planets gradually increase the inaccuracy so much that it will be as large as the Earth's orbit after this period of time. Thus, one is no longer able to predict, for a given date, whether there will be summer or winter. At first, this difficulty appears to be inconsequential, for couldn't one simply measure the Earth's position more exactly, in order to prolong the period of predictability? But how exactly must one observe the position of Earth in order to predict its position, say, in twice the period of time, in 240 million years? Answer: The present location of the Earth's center must be more accurately known not by a factor of two—that is, 7.5 centimeters—as in the linear case, but within one Ångstrom (10^{1-8} centimeters), approximately the diameter of an atom. Such is the difference between a linear system, in which the error of prediction increases linearly—that is, proportionally to time—and a chaotic system, in which the error grows exponentially.

Our inability to make exact prognoses is not simply a problem that a good engineer can solve through larger computers or better measurement. It lies in the mathematical properties of the physical equations. On the mathematical level, there are fundamental differences between simple (linear) and chaotic systems. The equations for the orbits of three heavenly bodies that attract each other are already so complex that they are unsolvable. And that is not because the mathematical statement was previously false, or because the theory of differential equations was too little developed.

The French mathematician Henri Poincaré had already proved in the nineteenth century that there can be no generally valid, exact solution. The difficulties increase with the number of bodies and the complexity of the theory. Nevertheless, almost exact calculations can also be made with a chaotic system, so long as the period of predictability is smaller than the exponential growth-time of the error. For the Earth's orbit, the growth-time is 4 million years. Then a doubling of the prediction period enlarges the error by a factor of 7.4, but a twentyfold prolongation increases the error by a factor of 500 million. The initial accuracy must be improved by this factor so that the deviation remains the same. One fights a losing battle against the exponent, which would demand immeasurable initial exactness for longer periods of predictability. Although the system is deterministic, we must admit that its development is *de facto* unpredictable.

What is amazing about the chaotic nature of Earth's orbit is that we notice it so little. Since 4.6 billion years, the orbit has changed chaotically, to be sure, but not substantially. It has always remained only weakly elliptical and at approximately the same distance from the Sun. With certain planetoids between Mars and Jupiter, this is not so. The American astronomer Daniel Kirkwood already determined in 1867 that the orbits of the planetoids are not exactly accidental. In a 2.5 fold orbital radius of the Earth, strikingly few planetoids revolve. At this distance, the period of rotation equals exactly one-third of that of Jupiter, the mightiest planet. If Jupiter completed one rotation, a planetoid would have circled the Sun exactly three times. Kirkwood also found similar gaps at the periods' proportions of 2:1, 4:1, and 5:2. These integer proportions are termed resonances. The phenomenon was not explained until the rise of chaos theory.

In 1981, a doctoral student at the California Institute of Technology, Jack Wisdom, used a powerful computer to calculate the orbits of planetoids in resonance. He could show that their orbits are chaotic and change substantially and unpredictably as a result of the simultaneous attraction of Jupiter and the Sun. Orbits in resonance are especially favorable for the transmission of momentum and energy between the planet and the planetoid. Wisdom found that the resonant orbits now and then become strongly elliptical and cross the orbits of planets closer to the Sun, of Mars in particular, and less often of the Earth. It can happen, then, that the resonant planetoid strikes one of these planets or is so deflected that it escapes the solar system and gets lost in interstellar space. Resonant planetoids have become rarer as a result and are missing from the statistics. This explains Kirkwood's gaps.

The collision of a planetoid with Earth would be one of the greatest natural catastrophes imaginable. The 3:1 gap is not yet completely empty. At least two larger planetoids, Alina and Quetzalcoatl, are in resonance with Jupiter. That is also probably valid for the planetoid 1989AC, which will approach Earth in its strongly elliptical orbit in the year 2004 at a distance of one and a half million kilometers, four times the distance to the Moon. Chaos in the solar system means that one cannot calculate thousands of years ahead which planetoid will actually be the next to hit the Earth.

A familiar chaotic system is the Earth's weather. It is once again the large number of equations concerning different, interacting air masses that makes long-term prognoses impossible. We shall never know the weather a year in advance, although the relevant processes in the Earth's atmosphere are well known. In fact, almost all of the processes in the universe are chaotic, particularly systems that are not in equilibrium. The only exceptions are arrangements that are especially simple or made so, like the classical swinging pendulum in school experiments, a single particle in an accelerator, or a mechanical machine. One cannot predict, in the long run, the exact condition of complex systems as they tend to occur in nature. Yet chaos does not rule in unlimited fashion; certain prognoses remain completely possible. In closed chaotic systems, symmetries and conservation laws like energy conservation are valid. Within the general framework of the conservation laws, however, the system can assume in principle any arbitrary state, and its details cannot be predicted.

Insight into the chaotic character of nature lowers certain expectations raised by the age of Enlightenment. In the eighteenth century, scientists had pictured the cosmos as a machine, in which individual parts fit together like the gears of a clock according to its given design. If a gear turns at a certain angle, another one rotates the predetermined amount. If the first gear turns at double the angle's size, the angle of rotation of the second gear doubles also. This view of the universe was, without a doubt, linear.

The nonlinear mutual interactions determining the current view of the universe do not fit the clockwork image and a fixed design plan. The cosmos does remain rational, for a chaotic system is deterministic, even when its rationality cannot be wholly expressed mathematically and is not predictable in the long term. However, our worldview, including physical aspects of the human body, must adapt to this new concept of the chaotic. The clockwork paradigm is outdated as a worldview. As a new example and model, a hurricane could serve, because it spontaneously arises out of fluctuations in the Earth's atmosphere and its development can be predicted only briefly. There is simply no blueprint for the formation of such a low pressure system. Perhaps a butterfly fluttered its wings, or somebody had whispered a tender word of love. A small gust of wind in an unstable location is enough to set a self-amplifying process in motion and to change the weather completely. Of course this little flurry of wind is only one of a billion others; it is also only the local and accidental trigger, not the cause of the change. The cause is the globally unstable weather condition.

The formation of stars and planets, biological development, the origin of the human species, the history of civilization and of the individual—all these processes are assuredly of this chaotic kind. It is never possible to predict their long-term future.

Chaos means that a small displacement of the original location can put the system onto another course and comprehensively alter its distant future. Since we do not exactly know the initial location, the future is not calculable in the long term and is therefore open. The result of chaotic processes often appears accidental to us, as for instance the die illustrates. Although I can make all kinds of efforts to throw the die exactly the same way, the result proves to be different every time. How can a deterministic process be open to chance? Chance plays along already at the very outset of the process, with the choice of the initial course. The initial conditions are, however, not of unique import, for a slight disturbance at any later moment can also alter the path and produce a significantly different outcome. In the die example, the initial position of the hand and its speed, the form and composition of the die, as well as the surface of the table where the die bounces all influence the outcome. Quantum mechanical uncertainty may add to the unpredictability of the process.

Corresponding to the unpredictable future of a chaotic system, its past is also cloaked in darkness. The past year's weather cannot be calculated in detail, either. Since the present is not completely predetermined, the past thus loses significance. The beginning can no longer be regarded as the dictator of all that follows.

Self-organization without Self

Self-organization denotes the development of a system into an order that is independent of special initial conditions. The term "self-organization" derives from chemistry, where certain reactions accelerate nonlinearly and cause a spatial pattern.[53] The principle of the chemical reactions can be described with mathematical precision, even if the spatial structures result each time in something a bit different due to different initial conditions. The concept is easy to transfer to processes in physics and astronomy with similar equations. The formation of stars is one example. Similar cases are clouds in the sky, atmospheric low-pressure systems, or catalytic reactions of prebiotic chemistry. In biology, sociology, or even psychology, the mathematical models are no longer exact, and the concept of self-organization is, accordingly, defined differently or is understood more metaphorically.

Amplifying feedback is a distinctive characteristic of self-organization. As the initially small structure is strengthened, it again effects further growth. Self-organizing processes are nonlinear and do not amplify all of the initial signals equally. Mostly it is the largest fluctuations that attract all available energy toward themselves and then grow further.

When we speak of self-organization in the universe, we do not suppose that the universe has an independent self or personality. Another common misperception is to imagine a self of the new structure that creates this development autonomously. On the contrary, the example of star formation offers a clear illustration of what is meant by "self." If a somewhat denser region forms in an interstellar cloud through a slight disturbance, this region attracts gas from the surroundings. The denser region then dominates the attraction in an ever-larger space and accumulates more and more mass. The propellant force for the formation of the new structure derives only slightly from the initial fluctuation in density of the chaotic material, from which the star formed. The free gravitational energy is initially spread over all the gas in the entire interstellar cloud. This larger whole delivers the energy for the feedback effect. In other cases, the energy comes from outside, or the self-organization is triggered from the outside. In no case is a self-organizing system closed. The "self" of self-strengthening and self-organization only signifies that the development is not forced or controlled by external factors.

Another property of self-organizing processes in this connection is their final independence from details of the initial condition. Unlike a clock which is made by the clockmaker at the beginning and set into motion, the order of a self-organizing process forms only in the course of development. The "self" in the name also signifies independence from special conditions at the outset with which these processes set a course for an attractor. Thus, the equilibrium of a star can be attained from almost arbitrary points of departure concerning density fluctuations of the interstellar medium. Attractors are often quasi-stationary states, in which constructing and destructive processes maintain balance. Although the word "attractor" implies a goal that is inherent to the matter and toward which the system steers, the details of these processes are causal. As with the second law of thermodynamics and discussion of the fine tuning of the universe, we conclude that such teleology and causality do not exclude one another.

Openness and Freedom

Great changes in the worldview of physics throughout the twentieth century have thoroughly shaken the mechanistic view of the sciences. In the earlier image of the universe as clockwork, there was no place for openness. The future appeared to be decided right from the beginning. That outlook has changed as a result of quantum mechanics and nonlinear dynamics. Chance and chaos hamper long-term predictions. Are chance and chaos the material causes of openness? At first glance, these principles still seem to contradict the freedom of humanity or the openness of human history. An electron is not free. Even when chance presents a striking contrast to the customary determinism, the electron cannot make a decision. Concerning chance processes, it is bound by the law of large numbers. A group of particles can organize themselves, but self-organization does not mean autarchy. On the contrary, self-organization is often based on energy that is drawn in from the outside and heat that is led away. Self-organization also does not signify arbitrariness, for a definite end-condition stands ahead, the so-called attractor, which seemingly guides the process "to itself."

As a physicist, I ask myself how I can have a free will and thus be responsible for my decisions, when apparently all of the atoms in my brain function according to causal laws. Chance and chaos do not imply the complete rejection of determinism; nevertheless, they open up new dimensions in the worldview of physics. Are chance and chaos, then, the long-sought material preconditions for freedom? With this question, we make a bold leap to the other side of the chasm, where Pericles maintained: "The secret of freedom is courage." He would certainly not be content with chance and chaos. Freedom, courage, and hope are spiritual values that influence our lives, even in the case of scientists. These values are associated with one another, depend upon one another, and have in common the fact that they are not realized through matter alone. That point is already evident insofar as not every human being is free. None is completely free; freedom must often be fought for. Because of our dependence on our surroundings, freedom is often limited, or in other cases may be considered an undeserved treasure.

Although the basic laws of physics are extremely simple, their consequences can be unimaginably complex. The variety of the universe and its openness come about through the nonlinear, chaotic, and random character of these consequences. It is also fascinating to notice how these newly discovered qualities of matter bring the sciences closer to spiritual values. Spiritual values are based on thoughts, whose physical reality also expresses itself in measurable brain waves. These currents, moreover, are based on quantum mechanical effects at the level of molecules and elementary particles. There are no direct connections, to be sure, but correspondences are indeed recognizable. They make it noticeably easier for a scientist like me to reflect upon openness and freedom.

THE FUTURE OF THE UNIVERSE

About four thousand years ago, Egyptian astronomers made the first known predictions about the seasons and the flooding of the Nile. Starting around 700 B.C., the Babylonians could predict eclipses of the Moon and Sun. In astronomy today, future orbits of planets, ebb and flow, the precession of the Earth's axis, the orbits of space probes, occultations of binary stars, and much more can be predicted. We rely daily on scientific predictions, whether directed toward the reliability of concrete building materials, material fatigue in airplane parts, or tomorrow's thunderstorm. Predictions of future happenings are merely projections to be verified or rejected after the event has occurred. In the field of astrophysics, we cannot always wait for this. Among many possible prognoses, those must be selected that have proved most successful in the past. Scientific predictions are similar to explanations of past events and thus are models based on known facts and experiences. They claim to be neither wholly reliable nor absolutely true. It is hardly surprising, then, that scientific literature about the future of the universe is scarce. That which deals with the farthest time to come is as speculative as the theories of the beginning.

There are no prognoses without assumptions. The simplest weather prediction is the assumption of persistence: it will remain as it is. That holds for weather patterns over a few hours, and often over one or two days, but seldom for longer periods. A better prediction is achieved with the assumption that it is not the condition which lasts but that certain laws remain operable so as to generate the conditions. The natural laws are well known that describe atmospheric currents, cloud formation, and condensation into snow and rain. On the basis of observed weather patterns, large computers can calculate weather developments in advance. The results are the known weather prognoses, with their sometimes disappointing reliability.

Equations concerning the Earth's atmosphere are nonlinear to a large degree so that, as was shown in the previous chapter, long-term predictions are not possible. Nonetheless, extremes can be postulated based on the laws of conservation, especially that of energy. It is, for instance, impossible for present solar irradiation to heat any given point on the Earth's surface above 100° C. This result of model calculations agrees with observations on petrified plants and animals from the past 3.5 billion years. With the exception of simple thermophilic bacteria, none of these forms of life would have survived a higher temperature. Even the laws of conservation are not beyond doubt, for they are derived from limited experiences, and perhaps we simply do not know all the factors that determine the distant future. For our prognoses, though, we accept the laws of conservation as an "iron framework" within which it is possible to see development as in some measure "open."

Sun and Earth Will Pass Away

How long the Sun will continue to shine can be predicted more surely than the weather in the coming month. The Sun originally contained $1.5 \cdot 10^{27}$ tons of hydrogen. With its fusion of four atomic nuclei of hydrogen to one helium nucleus, about one-hundredth of the mass is released as energy. A simple calculation shows that this energy supply will suffice to power the present luminosity for 81 billion years. Even so, the Sun has already changed since its formation 4.6 billion years ago. So far, hydrogen has fused only in the innermost part of the Sun, the core. If even a small percentage of the hydrogen is used up, as is the case with the Sun today, the star's structure changes. The core, enriched by helium, becomes denser and hotter. Both conditions accelerate nuclear fusion and cause it to produce more heat. The star's surface expands, the luminosity increases, and the lifetime is shortened. As soon as about 10 percent of the hydrogen is exhausted, this development becomes faster and faster, and uses up the energy supply in a much shorter time than in the previously mentioned period. The aging star becomes so large that its surface cools and becomes reddish. It arrives at the well-known red giant phase and, in a grand finale, burns up the larger portion of its energy supply in a short time.

The numerical simulations concur fairly well with the observations of stars similar to the Sun, those which are further along in their development or younger than our Sun. Another way to check predictions using star clusters, where all stars have approximately the same age, has been previously described. Stars having different mass develop at different speeds and today present themselves in different evolutionary states. An impressive example is the globular star cluster 47 Tucanae, about ten billion years old, in which all of the stars having one solar mass are in the process of becoming red giants. The more massive stars have reached that phase already, and the most massive ones have long since become white dwarfs, neutron stars, or black holes.

The luminosity of the Sun has already increased by 40 percent since its formation. In another 5.5 billion years, the luminosity will double in comparison with the present value. In the following 300,000 years, the core will shrink, the hydrogen fusion will shift to a shell around the core, and the color of the surface will change to red. Within a further billion years, the luminosity will increase by a factor of one thousand.

As a red giant, the Sun will have a totally different core than at present. Its matter will be a strange state, since the density will equal about ten kilograms per cubic centimeter. For this reason, the electron gas will be degenerate and conduct the temperature so well that it will be the same everywhere in the core. If the core now shrinks further and the temperature exceeds 100 million° C, the nuclei of helium atoms will fuse into nuclei of carbon and oxygen. Because of the uniformity of temperature, this reaction will begin almost simultaneously in the entire core and run its course within a few centuries. This so-called helium-flash will only occur in the core. Thirty million years will pass before the produced heat will visibly change the surface. The Sun will then expand one last time and attain its maximal size of one hundred times the current diameter; its luminosity will exceed the present value by a factor of two thousand. In this phase, a planetary nebula may form (Fig. 7). The Sun's outermost layer will detach and expand as a blue-red shining shell into interstellar space. For thirty thousand years, it will be a fantastic sight for any onlookers in the entire Milky Way.

Then the Sun will fill the space up to the orbit of Venus. Both Mercury and Venus will vaporize in its hot gases. On the Earth, the Sun will

Figure 7: The shell of the Helix Nebula, 450 light years away, has a diameter of four light years. Exactly in the center an old star is visible, today a white dwarf, which 20,000 years ago threw off its outermost layer as planetary nebula (Photo: ESO).

cover a third of the sky by day and send out heat that will scorch everything. All of the oceans will boil off; most of the steam and the air will escape into space. The surface temperature will be over 1,500° C, so that even rock will partially melt. No life will endure on the Earth; neither thermophilic bacteria nor viruses will survive. Even the traces of life will be extinguished.

At this time, it will also become hot in the outer solar system. At the distance of Pluto, the radiation of the Sun will still exceed that which, at present, reaches the Earth. Pluto's ice armor of methane and water will melt, and perhaps a colony of emigrated humans will establish a new civilization. We cannot forget, however, that the genus of Homo has substantially developed both physically and intellectually only within the last million years. Our species of Homo sapiens evolved just about 200,000 years ago. The colonists in 6.8 billion years could change so much that they might hardly recognize us as fellow humans, should the evolution of humans proceed further at only a thousandth of its past rate.

After a few ten millions of years more, the Sun will shrink definitively. Its surface will heat up through the contraction and become white. The Sun will become a white dwarf star, with a diameter like that of Earth; its density will be one ton per cubic centimeter. The luminosity will only be a ten-thousandth of what it is today, so that the solar system will become ice cold. The Earth will cool down to the temperature of space, -270° C. There will no longer be a planet for refuge, unless the future living beings build one in the proximity of the Sun. In 100 trillion years (10^{14}), the Sun will be wholly frigid. It will then no longer be a gas ball as it is today but will solidify to a crystallike material, a sphere as large as the Earth with a gaseous atmosphere of a few meters' thickness. People could not live there, for the gravity will exceed by a hundred thousand times that of the Earth and would flatten humans to the ground.

The Universe Will Not Remain as It Is

Will the universe exist at all in 100 trillion years, ten thousand times its present age? According to current knowledge about natural processes, that depends on whether cosmic expansion continues or whether the mass of the entire universe is sufficient to reverse this movement and to bring it into collapse. As we have seen, the answer is still controversial. On the one hand, the density of the stars and gas clouds—the self-illuminating, visible masses—is almost one hundred times too small to stop the expansion. The mass of the galaxies that is required to explain the revolution rates of distant globular clusters and of satellite galaxies, which also includes the invisible mass, is still too small by a factor of ten. These numbers have not substantially altered for more than thirty years. On the other hand, the inflation model of the early universe predicts the border case between collapse and eternal expansion.

Most theoreticians suppose that the missing 90 percent of mass will still be found, perhaps in the form of neutrinos or still unknown elementary particles or as vacuum energy. According to this model of critical mass density, the view prevalent among experts today, the universe would expand infinitely, but at an ever-slower rate. In the mathematically ideal case, it would come to a standstill after an infinite period of time.

The difference between observed and theoretically predicted mass density could also be explained by assuming that we live in a part of the universe that is below average in density. This part would expand without end, while other parts could collapse into giant black holes, out of which nothing could escape, not even signs of life in the form of electromagnetic emissions.

The future of cosmic expansion is unclear enough that some still pursue theories of universal collapse. A million years before the "Big Crunch," as it is described in pictorially sinister terms, the cosmic background radiation would become so intense that all life would burn up as if in a microwave oven. It is imaginable that the universe would finally plunge again into the vacuum from which it perhaps originated, and disappear. One could not differentiate it in any way from the primeval vacuum before the universe. Some have also envisioned models of a periodically pulsating universe that would expand again after each collapse. There is not much evidence for this theory, either in physics or in astronomy, and such scenarios remain extremely speculative. It is thinkable, however, that from the state of vacuum a new universe would, at some time, arise again spontaneously.

I hold to the assumption supported best by observation: that the universe will eventually expand without limit. Gravitation, then, has the general tendency to structure the material of the universe, forming it into galaxies, stars, or black holes. There is enough hydrogen in our galaxy, the Milky Way, to empower star production for another ten trillion (10^{13}) years. Even stars that are extremely long-lived, having a smaller mass than the Sun, will all contract to white dwarfs in 10^{14} years. How much longer new stars will still form depends upon the nature of invisible matter. Accounts on this duration are still inexact. Nevertheless, it seems plausible that at some point in time the hydrogen supply will be used up and no new stars will form.

The orbit of the Sun is chaotic among the jumble of two hundred billion other stars and cannot be calculated in the long term. On its way around the galactic center, the Sun will encounter other stars. At some time in the future, the minimal distance to a neighboring star will be so small that the planetary orbits will be noticeably disturbed. Should two stars approach within roughly the distance defined by the radius of a planetary orbit, it could happen that the planet detaches from its mother star and crosses over to the other, or gets lost into interstellar space. The average period of time for another star to come so close that the Earth could separate from the Sun and catapult into space is 10^{15} years. After one hundred such encounters, all the planets around a star will be hurled away with great certainty. In less than 10^{17} years, the Earth will draw a solitary orbit in the Milky Way, if it does not receive so much additional momentum that it is flung out of the galaxy. Less probable and less frequent are encounters that could divert the Sun itself out of its orbit. By very close encounters, it could experience so much acceleration that it, too, is thrown out of the Milky Way. It is much more likely though that the Sun will lose energy in the process and sink in the direction of the galactic center. The common effect of many close encounters slows the galactic rotation and causes the disk of the Milky Way to contract. This effect is the same as the evaporation of a liquid: the fastest particles leave the surface, and the fluid of the remaining particles cools down. The process is also observed in globular star clusters and is well known. After 10^{19} years, this process will be so advanced that most stars and planets, including the Sun and Earth, are either irretrievably buried in the central black hole of the Milky Way or else wind their way through intergalactic space as "vaporized" single bodies.

The matter of the atomic nucleus is not stable in the long term. It is the same unified theory—unconfirmed to be sure—of the interaction of elementary particles, upon which cosmic inflation is based, that also predicts the disintegration of protons with a half-life period of about 10^{33} years. Protons are whirling balls of two up-quarks, one down-quark, plus the field quanta, the gluons, that bind them together. Due to their quantum nature, the components can turn into other elementary particles for a short time. If their energy exceeds that of the protons, they must again unite within the time uncertainty. In all of this, the law of energy conservation functions like a strict auditor who always sees to it that the final account is correct. If the sum of their masses is smaller, the disintegration may be final. With the surplus energy, the new particles move away from each other. The quarks of a proton transform themselves about every 10^{33} years, into a π^0 (neutral pion) and a positron (antiparticle of electron), according to the theory mentioned above. The π^0 decays within a fraction of a second into either two highly energized photons or a photon, electron, and positron. The entire decay process is, in principle, reversible. Nevertheless, it is more and more improbable as time goes on that the newly formed particles will find themselves and reunite. It is the trend of the more probable which—as Ludwig Boltzmann interpreted the second law of thermodynamics—makes the progression of time irreversible. Out of the playful bubbling of the chaotic vacuum, some sober conclusions arise. Without interacting protons, neutrons and therewith all atomic nuclei will also be unstable. When protons decay, all constituent building blocks of our macrocosmos will deteriorate also. After about two hundred half-life periods, in perhaps 10^{35} years, the last nucleon will have decayed.

The matter of the universe will then continue to exist as thin gas made up of photons and leptons—these are mostly electrons, positrons, and neutrinos—blowing around a framework of supermassive black holes. Black holes are perhaps also unstable and radiate the entire energy contained in their mass, until they disappear completely. In 1974, Stephen Hawking suggested the process resting on a quantum mechanical effect, whereby particles—above all, photons—could "tunnel through" under the limb of the black hole, since their location is uncertain. The process is so slow that it will take 10^{100} years until a large black hole with the mass of a galaxy is radiated away.

The outlook over the distant future of the universe, under the assumptions of presently known natural laws, is certainly speculative. We do not yet know the universe and the laws of conservation well enough to foretell even crudely the future over more than a few tens of billions of years. Only the future of the Sun is reliably known, and its development appears to be symptomatic for the whole universe. The solar system will change drastically, due to the finite energy supply of the Sun; the Earth will no longer be habitable in today's way—at first too hot, and then too cold—for each form of life known to us. The development of the universe will surely continue. Will life, and particularly its expression in the species of human beings, be able to adapt to this future development? Or will humanity, one of many chapters in the universe's development, also come to an end?

ANOTHER VIEW OF THE FUTURE

T hus far we have coolly been examining prognoses about the future. Not only global changes but destruction of the foundations for life, including the possible extinction of all life in its present form, can be predicted according to exact scientific models. But even when these prognoses concern the distant future, I cannot write about them without some feeling of horror. The future reality does affect us, for, as human beings we are inevitably drawn to ponder the whole story of the universe's development in all its openness and uncertainty.

Earlier generations were also familiar with such anxiety in the face of destruction. What produced their anxiety was not astrophysics but rather the threat of plagues, war, death, or the annihilation of social order. This chapter describes a religious perspective on feelings about the future. I will consider here how anxiety toward threatening perils and crises was addressed in the New Testament. This brings us to the notion of *hope*. It has remained the most striking attitude toward the future for almost two thousand years, even through persecution, upheavals, and wars. Upon what is this hope based? In the following, the *"I am"* sayings of the Forth Gospel will be introduced, which express Christian hope and illustrate it in exemplary fashion.

"I am" Sayings

In the Gospel according to John, Jesus makes statements about himself that are unique in the New Testament. They have a typical form with two parts. All begin with "I am," followed by an image: the bread of life—the true vine—the good shepherd—the gate—the light of the world—the way, the truth, and the life—the resurrection and the life. After this first section of identification, there follows an invitation: "Come to me" or "He who comes to me," and a promise: "he will not hunger—will bear fruit—find pasture—not live in darkness—not be lost—live." At the conclusion of this book, I shall try to formulate a similar I-am image, in the manner of Jesus, which summarizes my reflections about the future.

Little is known about the origin of the I-am sayings. The Gospel of John is undoubtedly the youngest of the four in the biblical canon and was written down around the year 100 A.D. The Gospels arose in different locations, each with its own tradition. In each setting, the sayings of and about Jesus were preserved, stories were collected, and already the first narratives were shaped. A culture of hymns, phrases, and creeds developed in worship. The evangelists chose from these sources. In doing so, the first three Gospels still strongly retain the form of a narration. They are constructed rather like a biography. The story begins with the birth or baptism of Jesus, goes on to describe his teaching activity in Galilee, and culminates in Good Friday and Easter. The author of John's Gospel also follows a biographical pattern, but gave his text a more logical, conceptualized structure. In this way, the Gospel is less a story and more reminiscent of a modern research report, in which observations are not simply recorded but selectively apprehended, collated, and interpreted. "The consciously working, extremely competent author, who has command over a broad spectrum of ways to form and shape,[54] concentrated above all on the words of Jesus. The I-am sayings are defining points in this logically ordered testimony.

Because of their uniqueness and stylistic uniformity, it is obvious that the I-am words stem from a single source to which only the author had access, or, because they correspond to the theology of John precisely, that he himself wrote them down for the first time. The contents remind one of Old Testament and Jewish apocalyptic texts. Yet an I-am revelation in pictorial form is not to be found in the Old Testament nor in Judaic or Qumran texts of that time.[55] The linguistic feature of pictorial parallels is, however, known from gnosticism, a speculative religious philosophy of Hellenism.

Today, New Testament experts generally agree that the I-am sayings are not word-for-word quotations of Jesus. That point will also be assumed in what follows, but is not decisive. Much more significant is the assumption that they are well-reflected summaries of his message. That message could no longer be handed down in literal historical citations at the time of John, since the original language and culture became less and less understandable with the passage of time. In the interval between Easter and the writing of John's Gospel, much had changed in the eastern Mediterranean region. Jerusalem was destroyed, the Christian communities persecuted and dispersed. Most of all, the gospel writer had to convey the Aramaic words of Jesus in terms meaningful to his audience of Greek-speaking Jewish Christians, living in a Hellenistic environment. If he had merely transmitted the stirring message of Jesus seventy years later in some literal form, he might have interested his listeners historically, but would no longer have addressed them personally. John wanted to make this message understandable with expressions familiar to those living three generations after Jesus.

The I-am words relate directly to the central religious experience of Moses. In the story of the burning bush, God proclaims God's name—and with it, God's innermost nature—*Ehyeh asher ehyeh* ("I am who I am," or, more relevant for our purpose, "I will be, who I will be." Exodus 3:14.) From the "I-am" as associated with the third-person form "he-is," the Hebraic name for God, "Yahweh," originated.[56] Also, the curious form of the I-am sayings in the original Greek text, *ego eimi* instead of only the standard form *eimi*, refers back to the Old Testament. An *ego* ("I") stands before the Greek verb, which already contains the personal pronoun as in the present-day Italian or Spanish. This striking form of speech emphasizes the speaker, but hints also of its origin in the Semitic languages.

The figurative form of the I-am formula already makes clear that something wants to be said which lies behind appearances in the foreground. Obviously, Jesus is not chemically similar to bread when he declares "I am the bread of life," but in his manner of satiating, he is bread indeed. However, we are not only dealing with a simple metaphor or simile (not just a comparison: I am *like* bread, *like* a shepherd, and so forth). Most of all, the sayings wish to express that in everything that satiates, that quenches thirst, and that points in the right direction, Jesus can be perceived. That is, Jesus is to be experienced in any piece of bread. At this point, of course, "Jesus" does not refer only to the historic person from Nazareth, but to a cosmic principle that transcends him.

Moreover, the uniqueness of Jesus is stressed: Jesus alone is the true bread, the good shepherd, and so forth, in contrast to worldly satiety and to other figures of redemption. The exclusivity and insistence of the claim may sound perplexing. Its meaning can only be explained in relation to the way in which the Johannine author and perhaps Jesus himself understood Jesus' mission. Already for many of his original listeners, such utterances were felt to be an annoyance or a deliberate provocation. According to John it cannot be otherwise when the divine penetrates somebody's immediate experience instead of remaining at a metaphysical distance.

The I-am sayings are not meant to scandalize but to proclaim redemption and—what is essential here—to communicate hope. They address the various forms of privation that create evolutionary pressure on human beings. In face of elementary deprivation—lack of food and security—humanity's desire for a life unthreatened by the vicissitudes of time is evident. These figurative sayings point out that the real miracle is not the multiplication of the loaves offering temporary satiety; rather, I-am sayings refer to a future fulfillment. Moreover, this eschatological reality can already be experienced now. The surprised listeners are told that the true bread already exists. The sayings of bread, vine, shepherd, light, truth, and life proclaim redemption in turn from hunger, barrenness, loss of direction, darkness, delusion, and death. And redemption does not take place wholly in the future but begins now. According to John, Jesus identifies himself with the unprecedented claim of eschatological hopes realized here and now.

For John, the heart of the gospel is that the "word" involves not merely a literal formula but a power capable of changing the world. Significantly, John describes Jesus in the Logos hymn[57] that opens his Gospel as the one, creative word of God (Greek *logos*). The I-am formulas condense the historical sayings and teachings of Jesus in a manner accessible to later generations. Thus his words again assume their original vigor, capable of effecting change. That the Gospel of John found acceptance in the biblical canon despite its late appearance and became a book in the New Testament confirms the ready response to this new formulation of Jesus' message in a cultural climate shaped by Hellenism.

Christological Interpretations as Models

Besides intending to propagate and concentrate the tradition, the author of John's Gospel shows a strong interest in *interpreting* the events concerning Jesus. In his famous prolog, they are set in cosmological terms. The sayings of Jesus sometimes change abruptly into an interpretation of Jesus. A report, as objective as possible, about the historical Jesus may be very important to us living today. But this keen interest in factual description first developed in modern times. The ancient historians wanted to spare later and uninformed readers the effort of evaluating and interpreting what happened. For the early Christians, it was also much more important to understand and to proclaim what the life and death of Jesus signified, than it was to communicate biographical details. Inspired by the message of Jesus, the author of John's Gospel made this teaching available again for his time by introducing his own bold interpretation. His work could be a model for the manner in which this message is appropriated.

A religious interpretation or theology has some similarities with a scientific theory or model. It is not to be understood as the absolute truth but as an attempt to approach the truth as closely as possible. Perhaps there is a deeper reason why the Greek stem of the word "theory" (*theoreo* Greek = to view, consider, appreciate) is similar to the word for God, *theos*. Interpretations are necessary because the facts alone—as, for instance, those related to the life and death of Jesus so far as they are accessible—cannot be assembled into an integral whole. We term interpretations of the story of Jesus, as rendered by John and others, *christological models*.

I-am sayings are condensed christological models. Their abstractness calls to mind formulas in physics. It must immediately be pointed out, however, that there are also important differences from scientific models. The I-am sayings make no sense in purely formal terms. The subject of the sentence, Jesus, does not materially correspond to the predicated substances of bread, wine, and so forth. Obviously, the I-am words are neither mathematical equations nor chemical formulas, and do not answer a "what" question, as is the case in scientific statements. Even more significant is the fact that a scientific expression, as mentioned earlier, relates only to objects. The subject, with his or her feelings, expectations, and hopes, steps completely into the background. The object is examined and condemned to passivity. In contrast, the I-am sayings aim to produce a relation among four poles: first, with Jesus and therefore with God; second, with the addressed human being; third, with the person's distress and needs; and fourth, with the prospect of surmounting these deficiencies, metaphorically represented through bread, wine, and so forth. All four points must be in the picture in order to understand the model. The aptness of such a message, which aims to establish a relationship, cannot be affirmed through an objective, indifferent observation. Only those who open themselves up to the message and who allow the relation to develop can test the truth of the I-am sayings.

I-am sayings are condensed interpretations of inherited experiences at the level of faith. They contain interpretations of Jesus' historical life, of his violent death, and of his appearances after Easter. There are other interpretations of the same stories. It is instructive to compare them in the following paragraphs.

In his lifetime, Jesus was taken to be the Messiah by his followers. The Greek word stems from the Hebrew *maschiach* (Greek = *christos*) and means "anointed one." In the Old Testament, this is the general designation for the kings of Israel, later also for the high priests, whose heads were rubbed with oil at their inauguration. In Jesus' time and under Roman rule, the Messiah denoted the promised king, whose kingdom would restore the national sovereignty of Israel and include the whole world. The Gospels typically showed Jesus himself reluctant to claim this identity explicitly. Nevertheless, it seems he did understand his role to be one of conveying a salvation affecting the future of all humankind.

John's environment of Hellenistic Jewish Christians in the Middle East was disposed to interpret Jesus, or the resurrected Christ, as God's "wisdom" or "reason." Wisdom as a characteristic of God was also revered in early Jewish-Gnostic speculation and personified mythically. Wisdom was, at the beginning, with God and proceeded from God. Indeed through God's wisdom, God created the cosmos. Jesus was identified with Wisdom; through him, Wisdom was directly perceivable. This interpretation is evident above all in the prolog to the Gospel of John, the Logos hymn to Wisdom as the divine word of creation.

In modern times, Pierre Teilhard de Chardin interpreted the person and acts of Jesus in relation to the evolutionary view of the universe. Teilhard saw the development of the universe and of humankind as part of a general convergence of cosmic evolution in the direction of higher consciousness involving ever-deeper awareness, of compassion and fellowship, so that the universe becomes more and more "christlike."

The interpretation of John—we could term it the "Logos" model— shows how the figure of Jesus already suggested a broader cosmic meaning for Christians of the ancient world that far exceeded the local and temporal framework of events in Jerusalem around 31 A.D. The first

Christians already perceived in Jesus a deeper dimension, through which they recognized anew the fundamental concepts of creation by which the entire cosmos had been created. The author of John's Gospel starts from the principle that no earthly term could capture the kind of reality encountered in Jesus. Therefore, he presents many I-am sayings with multiple images to illuminate repeatedly the same content from various perspectives. In addition, John applies a multitude of personal titles, from "Logos" to "Son of Man" and "Son of God," to Jesus throughout the Gospel.

The argument of this entire book might be encapsulated in this motto: *"I am the truly new. Whoever trusts in me, shares in a meaningful world, despite decay and death, even when the Sun burns out, the Earth spins off into space, and the universe disintegrates."* This motto is not founded on the historical Jesus. Could it nevertheless be true? Perhaps today, John would formulate the messsage of Jesus in this manner, to affirm that the future course of our own life and death, as well as that of the heavenly bodies and the universe, are not the sole and final reality. So, too, hunger, thirst, and powerlessness did not appear as the ultimate reality to John at the brink of the second century. What really counts is this experience of creativity, which establishes the hope that newness will somehow open once again in the future.

The motto is an attempt to express the Logos model in terms of modern science. The saying considers cosmic catastrophes that threaten from afar as an extreme example of current anxiety over the future. Like John's Gospel, it proceeds from objective data to a level calling for the reader's participation. It recognizes in scientific facts the same creative power that already has become pointedly visible in our world in the person of Jesus and will be increasingly perceivable in the future.

Note that there is a transition from one level to another. Significantly, the objective level does not disappear from view but remains in our field of vision as a reference and source of images. The rational understanding of such an operation is possible only from a standpoint outside and above both levels.

The point is not that the new, which may arise out of this decaying world in its openness, would be generated through direct divine intervention. The past development of the universe shows that the new can be explained subsequently according to scientific laws. In the religious perception, however, the dynamic of change reveals a basic source that feeds the world processes. The very core of this newness, which has begun to arise and is still coming to be, bears a transcendent character. Precisely in the world of physics with its symmetries, energy conservation, chance, causality, and irreversible time, the surprisingly new will form. Not every change shows duration and futurity, but only the true and really new. Future salvation from worldly pain and destruction has, according to John, the same basis as the resurrection story of Jesus of Nazareth. The pattern is the same in past and future. Future newness is already breaking into the world, he would say, if only we could perceive it.

As we have seen, religious perception is another view of reality, one made possible by faith. The new view is relational: it creates an association among the observer, the object, and God. In this way, it interjects the human being into a comprehensive whole. It does not involve a kind of X-ray shot, which would scrutinize objects to even greater depth, so that they might again be objectified and manipulated. On the contrary, the relational view opens onto the whole. It brings object and subject into a larger context that includes a transcendent dimension. From this viewpoint, the tissue of the world's meaning can be discerned and a system of values can originate. Not everything that comes about is good. Evil also enters the field of vision as that which hinders, negates, and destroys this newness. Yet the evil thus encountered is not really new, for according to Christian belief, it has no long-term future. Faith and new perception, faith and the apprehension of meaning in the whole, are now seen to be mutually dependent.

HOPE IN SPITE OF PREDICTIONS

We are at the brink of a new millennium and gaze out to an immense sea of time. What is coming? Is there a gleam of hope in the remote future? As we look toward the future, science and religion meet. Granted, what is hoped for does not follow inevitably from the factual data before us. Even if our hopes have a foundation, they are never certain. One could therefore criticize every hope as illusory. Still, a person who hopes does not dwell in a fantasy land if his or her hope is sufficiently grounded in reality. Even if we speak of "hope contrary to all reason," we must acknowledge that factual appearances do not define the whole of reality. Hopes are based upon promises, ideals or—as in the case of Christian hope, in contrast to scientific prognosis—on the perception of the world as creation in accord with a certain pattern.

In the previous chapter, we saw how the author of John's Gospel perceived a prototypical pattern of creation in the person of Jesus. We have already introduced the Good Friday–Easter paradigm. What is the character of this pattern, as reflected in the Good Friday–Easter sequence, and how might we recognize it in the physical world? Drawing on the precedent of biblical tradition, this last chapter tries to describe the scientific view of the future in the language of Christian faith. Even as the common future becomes here a meeting point for religion and science, it remains important to distinguish clearly one from the other. Only in figurative terms can the patterns from one plane of discourse be "translated" to the other. At this point, then, a few reflections about metaphoric expressions and about the distinctive patterns of science and of religion are in order.

Recognizing Reality

The ability to associate an object of immediate perception with one recalled from memory is an amazing achievement of the brain. How this phenomenal capacity, not confined to humans, was acquired in the course of evolution is still little known in detail. Organisms with acute sensory perception and reliable neural judgment certainly had an edge in the fight for survival. Pattern recognition is also an important concern of modern computer science. It involves, for example, inventing procedures to automatically recognize and assess certain objects in video images. Applications range from quality tests in mass production, robotic controls, and the classification of fruit to the evaluation of satellite photos of entire countries. The technique of pattern recognition consists of three steps: at first a prototype pattern is defined; then the image content of the probe is determined by reducing it to characteristic values; and finally these are compared to the characteristic values of the pattern.

It is amazing how very accurate our brain is in recognizing familiar faces. In this case, too, the image is reduced to characteristic values, such as the distance between the eyes, shape of the nose, and hair length. The brain then compares these details with the memorized pattern. If we encounter a person we know at too great a distance for the brain to assemble data for recognition, it usually does not produce a false identity. Rather it holds back until the person is near enough for characteristic values to be confirmed. Recognition of the face then follows quickly and is almost always correct. Computers have not yet attained this astonishing accuracy.

In the formation of new structures in the universe, a pattern can likewise be discerned. As we have observed in the case of star formation, planets similar to Earth can form out of a chaotic mixture of original gas and cinders expelled by old stars. Yet the "formation of newness from old" is not simply a spatial pattern, as in the previous example, but a sequence involving time. The new arises in the universe repeatedly, in many ways and forms. The very early universe transformed itself several times, and its matter took new states; later galaxies formed along with stars, planets, and life. The pattern is in no way contained in every process; whole branches of biological development, for instance, have become extinct and appear to have been evolutionary dead-ends. Of course, it is possible that the extinction of one species of animal was precisely the necessary requirement for the formation of a new type. The pattern would nevertheless become recognizable within a larger context.

The events of Good Friday and Easter are again a great deal more elusive. What finally changed the history of the world was imbued with the astonishment of Jesus' shocked disciples. They perceived these events on a participatory level and in the context of a previously established personal relationship. There are also patterns discernible on this level of perception. They are not fundamentally different from those presented by our scientific examples. In both instances, an "image content" is extracted from certain data or experience that can serve as a cognitive pattern for others.

The content of the Good Friday event is the violent destruction of the person of Jesus, followed by Easter and the postresurrectional manifestations, in which Jesus appears to his followers and disciples in a new form.[58] Through the following basic features, one could characterize the disciples' response to the experience and recognize it as a prototypical pattern on the level of participating perception and language:

1. The confused and chaotic situation of Good Friday, from which there is no "linear" progression and no immediate exit.
2. The unexpected resurrection of Jesus at Easter.
3. The continuity of old to new, in that Jesus is recognized in his personhood, his new body still bearing the wounds of the crucifixion.
4. Awareness that traces of this newness can already be perceived before Easter, especially as described retrospectively from a postresurrectional perspective.
5. Recognition that the new is not a passing firework display but has qualities of duration and ongoing presence into the future. A new order establishes itself in the midst of the old structures—above all in the life of the earliest Christians.

Let me offer some examples of where in the world this temporal pattern on the level of participating perception can be recognized. The pattern's first basic characteristic seems most conspicuous. Great political empires and whole continents, heavenly bodies, and even the universe—all decay. Our own life will have an end. We have become conscious of the possibility of global catastrophes; and diffuse end-of-the-world anxieties hang in the air in view of the new millennium. The second basic feature of the pattern can be recognized, for example, in a newborn child. Although expected for months, it enters as a surprise into the life of the parents. From the parental genes, perhaps not yet old but marked for obsolescence, a new combination arises that claims an enduring place in their life. Other examples are political solutions to wars or unexpected scientific and technical breakthroughs. The pattern of suffering, destruction, and death followed by newness, by life and awakening, is also experienced in the realm of personal life. Literature contains many stories of tragic relationships that end in disappointment, guilt, or despair, but from the ruins of which a hopeful new beginning arises.

These examples also illustrate the basic features of points three and four. The child's genetic code exists already as part of the parental genes. Children also assume the intellectual, social, and material inheritance of the parents, and thus effect a continuity between generations. Point four is also reflected in political events, whose precipitant conditions are present long before their actual occurrence. Not everything that comes about is really new. Much is only different or disappears again without a trace.

The fifth characteristic assumes a persisting element. Only that which strives toward such a future state and shows some degree of continuation is really new. What, on the contrary, is temporary, gives only the appearance of newness and has no future. The really new points toward a goal; it is a part of a comprehensive development and is therefore meaningful in this context.

In technical and scientific cases, the question whether a given phenomenon conforms to a standard pattern can be answered objectively from the given leeway for variations. On the level of participatory perceptions, the values are not quantitative and must be assessed qualitatively. The search for a pattern can sharpen our perception and heighten our awareness for interconnections. Unless they degenerate into rigid presuppositions, patterns help us interpret our perceptions both on the objective level of technical and scientific matters and on the plane of human values and relations. It is through such patterns, in fact, that we order our multifarious sensory impressions.

The Role of Metaphors

A figurative description that expresses one thing in terms of another is termed *metaphor* after the Greek word *metaphora* (transfer). Metaphors are useful to characterize a complex phenomenon with a well-known expression from another level of experience. The figurative transfer awakens certain associations and emphasizes certain aspects of perception. Metaphors are very suitable for describing and explaining religious perceptions, for they illuminate what is impossible to formulate with words, or fill a gap where there are no rational concepts.[59]

For instance, astrophysicists associate the concept of "star formation," involving observation of certain molecular clouds hundreds of light years away, with equations of magnetohydrodynamics, nuclear fusion, or else they recall the same pattern in the formation of galaxies. In a poem, on the other hand, star development could be a metaphor for the coming and going of our own existence. Similarly, in lecturing before the general public, I notice that nonprofessional people often comprehend scientific results to image a reality that includes themselves and that is perceived on another level. This other reality cannot be completely grasped in discursive language or equations, and can only be communicated through metaphors.

Patterns and metaphors need to be differentiated. In the case of pattern recognition through a computer, it is easy to see that the pattern can be apprehended only with the same type of data as the prototype and on the same level. Concerning the formation of a new star from unordered interstellar material, a pattern was described that had certain similarities to the Good Friday–Easter pattern.

Are these patterns comparable? In the scientific domain of the first pattern, participating perceptions and the emotional response—involving for example compassion—are missing. Thus the two patterns do not coincide completely. In particular, the scientific pattern for "the formation of newness" lacks the breath and emotional depth of the paschal events. The two patterns operate on different planes, but contain, nevertheless, some common elements and analogies.

The pattern for the formation of newness could well be a metaphor for the paschal events. One prerequisite for this transfer is that the metaphor is well enough known. That the formation of something qualitatively new, as in the case of biological life, is also full of riddles from the scientific standpoint, makes transfer to the religious plane all the more apt. The phenomenon of the new that arises under chaotic conditions can thus be metaphorically communicated in the domain of existential crises and developments: *Easter is like the formation of life on the early Earth, as the planet is bombarded with meteorites and comets, and laid waste by volcanoes.*

Let us clarify the difference between patterns and metaphors with a few more examples. In a *pattern*, a key example is repeated based on similar data and on the same level of discourse. The prototype and the sample are of the same nature. In temporal patterns, the same course of events occurs again and again in much the same way, as illustrated by the habits of a person. Temporal patterns also apply to the evolution of species, or to phenomena discussed in sociology and in history. The formation of newness is a pattern on the level of the sciences.

A *metaphor*, in contrast, provokes awareness of similarities between objects or events on different planes of reality. A supernova, for instance, in which an old star returns a large portion of its mass to interstellar space and thereby enables a new generation of stars to form, can be a metaphor for the way in which parents give vital energy and possession to their children. Unlike a pattern, a metaphorical image does not explain the cause of the process. The altruistic activity of the parents, whether from motives of familial love or from instinct imprinted through evolution, does not have the same causes and cannot be described through equations equivalent to those appropriate for a supernova. Metaphors can place an obscure phenomenon in another light but cannot explain it. All of this means that scientific findings and illustrations can offer a metaphoric ground for helping believers as well as others to appreciate the religious character of humanity's hope for newness. Still, scientific results cannot, in themselves, engender hope.

Time and Hope

Astrophysics in the twentieth century has revealed a view of reality that shows an astonishing dynamic across time and stupendous changes in the universe since the Big Bang and the formation of the Earth—all the way to disquieting prospects for the distant future. The sciences have forced human beings to relinquish the fantasy of occupying the center of the cosmos. Some writers have coined the Copernican worldview, and all further extensions that render humanity less and less prominent in relation to the universe, an "insult" to humanity. I find much more demeaning the way we must live within a linear time that strides mercilessly forward. Concepts from archaic and eastern cultures of a periodic renewal of the world, of an eternal return and a cyclical time, do not suit the worldview of contemporary science. Human beings are not only forced spatially from the center, but must content themselves with only a minuscule portion of time compared with stars and galaxies. The individual stands neither at the end nor outside cosmic development. Connected to this circumstance is the indignity of living in the midst of death and a cosmic history that largely illustrates decay rather than progress.

In this decaying world, however, new structures and orders arise spontaneously. They were not predictable or, at least, could only be suspected embryonically. In the new scientific view of the universe, the cosmos unfolds out of primordial particles in a fascinating succession of developmental leaps.

Is this innovative past a scientific ground for hope? On the basis of past development, a favorable future for humankind, or even for the individual, cannot be derived conclusively. True, on at least one planet in the universe, the Earth, an environment occurred where life could form and biological evolution could proceed to the formation of human society. Still, simple optimism is unwarranted, even if one ignores the countless victims of this development with its wrong turns and dead-ends. All prognoses of the future—whether for living creatures, planets, stars, galaxies, or the universe itself—reveal decay at the last. The Sun will become cold, the Earth will lose itself in space, and even the matter in the universe will decay into radiation. Still, it is quite imaginable that something unexpected could also arise in the future that would be as new as life on Earth was four billion years ago. This kind of newness certainly cannot be foretold, for such developments are nonlinear and chaotic. *There is no scientifically provable hope.*

A scientist could therefore shrug his shoulders and conclude that uncertainty must accompany an open future. Yet I wish to change perspectives once more to pursue the question of where Christian faith obtains its hope. Hope can only grow in a trusting relationship. Such trust involves a certain foreknowledge with which a person faces the future. It touches on the relationship between the subject and the world. On the basis of this relationship, reality is perceived in a different way than on the basis of scientific method. Hope, trust, and faith cannot be brought about by dogmas or metaphysical constructions, but must accord with one's own perceptions.

The Christian tradition does not postulate the sort of optimism in which the development of the world is seen as a straightforward progression toward the good and the reasonable. The last book of the Bible, the Revelation of John, expresses the Christian perspective in apocalyptic visions. Its hope lies no longer in protection from crisis, but rather in the formation of newness. Hope is established within a divine dimension of time—namely, its creativity. The I-am sayings of the Johannine Gospel contain the hopeful promise that the crisis—whether of hunger, thirst, disorientation, or death—will be overcome, but without specifying how this will occur in concrete terms. It is not easy for us scientifically-minded people to accept a hope for which there is no causal justification.[60] As with the concept of creation, the scientific "how" must recede into the background, where hope for the future is concerned.

In the New Testament, hope is based upon the revolutionary events of Good Friday and Easter.[61] What took place then, says hope, will occur again in some comparable fashion. The experience pattern of crisis and redemption has a historical precedent by which hope can be gauged at any time. It is not surprising if Christians always come back to that. Moreover, the transcendent basis for hope becomes obvious in this prototype, since the hope in question seems to run contrary to nature and reason. This cycle of experience is the pattern for hope in small things as well as in great. Christians hope for nothing less than newness in the realm of death and in a world of merciless evolution; in religious language, they hope for a new creation.

It is worth recalling that no objectively certain facts are available concerning the Easter event. The Good Friday–Easter pattern makes sense only on another level of perception—that participatory level, where subject and object meet in an interactive relationship and form a whole. So neither the pattern nor the hope can be regarded as objectified facts. Christian hope does not follow from an interpretation of nature independent of the observing person and cannot be physically confirmed. Like human freedom, hope is not compulsive, but is rather something like a gift that one can accept or not. Hope is no abstract idea, for ultimately hope becomes integral to one's humanity and changes nothing less than the condition of human life.

How does one arrive at such hope? In hope, religious experience expresses itself on the level of faith. Such experience formed originally from elements of sensory perception. It also includes relational, "interior" perceptions of wholeness, dreamlike visions, or sudden insights while completely conscious. I experience them sporadically and allusively in quiet moments of everyday life when, for a brief time, an intensive relationship suddenly arises in the normal foreground of experience. The traditional pattern helps to identify and to integrate these perceptions. Living with hope, I do not perceive time only as a sequence of causal processes or chance, and as an infinitesimally brief present. Once the hoped-for future enters the picture, time embraces duration. It is the duration of waiting until newness forms. Through attentive waiting, I occasionally discover foreshadowings and intimations of the future newness. But this kind of perception requires patience, and a willingness to develop a reciprocal relationship to reality.

> *Jesus says:*
> *I am the truly new.*
> *Whoever trusts in me*
> *shares in a meaningful world,*
> *despite decay and death,*
> *even when the Sun burns out,*
> *the Earth spins off into space*
> *and the universe disintegrates.*

ACKNOWLEDGMENTS

When an astrophysicist ventures beyond the usual bounds of his scholarship, he is glad for any help. I would like to thank the theologian Samuel Vollenweider of the University of Bern most deeply. During numerous conversations with him about science and New Testament scholarship, I have gained important insights. I am also most grateful to Elisabeth Benz, Walter Fesenbeckh, Maja Pfaendler, Alfred Ringli, and my scientific colleagues Kurt Dressler and Hans Moor, as well as the theologians and religious scholars Hans-Peter Hasenfratz, Markus Huppenbauer, Peter Suchla, and Hans Weder. They have all read through earlier versions of the manuscript and have made valuable suggestions. I have also received important inspiration in the Ecumenical Study Group on theology of creation in Lucerne and in the working group Nature-Science-God at the universities of Zurich.

Epilog to the English Translation

The English version is dedicated to John and Julia Gatta, who have initiated and inspired this book and encouraged its translation. The text was translated into English by Elizabeth Austin and John Gatta. I have taken this opportunity to thoroughly revise it.

NOTES

1. One example among many that could be cited is *God and the New Physics* (London: J. M. Dent, 1983) by P. Davies, who renounces all religious experience and develops a concept for the term "God" on the basis of physical theories and with analogies to human comprehension. Consequently he states that "science offers a surer path to God than religion."

2. In order to heighten the spatial resolution and sensitivity of radio telescopes, single telescopes are coupled to interferometers. The most important and largest one in the world is the Very Large Array, which consists of twenty-seven telescopes, distributed over a surface diameter of 42 kilometers.

3. The ring of Saturn—composed of ice, pebbles, and rocks—is a kind of an accretion disk. It is slow in its development, since very little internal friction is present which could divert the angular momentum and enable the contraction to continue.

4. In ancient religious discourse, "chaos" signifies the ultimate threat to cosmic order. Out of chaos the cosmos has arisen and back into chaos it threatens to sink again. In terms of present-day physics, though, "chaos" is closer to the philosophical concept of contingency in which events, whether good or bad, are denoted that do not necessarily occur. The physical concept of chaos arose in opposition to the earlier image of a wholly predictable world. The impossibility of a detailed prognosis limits knowledge of the future and the technical applicability of science. From the standpoint of the older physics, "chaos" represents a breakdown of controllable order.

5. Most stars, including the Sun, constantly lose gas, which streams into space with great velocity: the stellar wind. The solar wind flows by the Earth and mixes with the interstellar gas at about a hundred times the Sun-Earth distance.

6. Black holes are regions of space with immense density of matter, and whose great gravitational pull allows it to hold everything back. No spaceship, no elementary particle, not even a photon can escape. When an object neither radiates nor allows light through, it appears black. Black holes emit at best a weak heat emission, which was postulated on the basis of a quantum mechanical effect. Objects of this

kind are predicted by theories of gravitation, especially the general theory of relativity as terminal points in the development of the most massive stars. Similar systems, though with millions of solar masses, are perhaps in the center of every galaxy.

7. The presence of radioactive aluminum in a certain kind of meteorite can only be explained through the explosion of a supernova in the immediate vicinity about a hundred million years before the formation of the solar system.

8. The term "Big Bang" has two meanings in use today. Some scientists use it to describe a model in which the universe expands like an explosion from a hot, dense condition about fourteen billion years ago. Others associate the term with a hypothetical singularity involving mathematically infinite density and temperature at the beginning of this expansion at zero time. In this book, the term is used according to its first and older meaning. The Big Bang scenario, but not the existence of a singularity is widely accepted by experts, even though certain details of the present standard model are thoroughly disputed.

9. The moving letter that Einstein wrote shortly before his death to the sister of a deceased, old friend may serve as an example: "He has now also preceded me with the parting from this strange world. This means nothing. For us physicists with faith, the separation between past, present, and future merely has the significance of an illusion, stubborn though it is." *Albert Einstein—Michele Besso, Correspondence 1903–1955* (Paris: Hermann, 1972).

10. By "system" we mean a number of objects which interact—for example, the planets of the solar system or the molecules in an atmosphere.

11. William R. Hamilton showed already in 1834 that a classical system is reversible when it is integrable—that is, when its general components of momentum are constants of motion. A derivation can be found, for example, in H. Goldstein, *Classical Mechanics* (Redding, Mass.: Addison-Wesley, 1959).

12. Since the beginning of modern physics, numerous researchers have occupied themselves with the apparent symmetry of time in the basic equations and its final irreversibility in reality. Newton had already noticed the reversibility of time in the basic equations. One can find an overview and newer aspects in the book by I. Prigogine and I. Stengers, *The End of Certainty: Time, Chaos, and the New Laws of Nature* (New York: Free Press, 1997).

13. The momentum is defined as the velocity times the mass of an object. In the case of very fast motions, the relativistic Lorenz factor plays an additional role.

14. Planck's constant was introduced by Max Planck in 1900 and has the dimension of energy times time. It appears in different connections in quantum mechanics.

15. In the Middle Ages, the ethical maxim to act as "if there were no God" (*etsi deus non daretur*) was introduced as an obligation not to wait for divine intervention. It was meant as a necessary principle to secure the rational structure of moral order.

16. I am adhering to the classical terminology by William James in *The Varieties of Religious Experience* (New York: Longmans, Green & Co., 1902).

17. Hans Weder remarks in ed. J. Audretsch, *Die andere Hälfte der Wahrheit* (Munich: C. H. Beck, 1992), p. 150: "With faith, thinking begins anew."

18. The German nineteenth-century poet Matthias Claudius wrote to his son: "Not the person is free, who can do what he wishes, but rather who wishes to do what he should."

19. According to the Christian belief, God has been revealed in the man, Jesus of Nazareth. Paul remarks, in the first Epistle to the Corinthians, that knowledge of this revelation is not learned, nor does it manifest itself through the study of philosophy. Rather, one is spoken to: "[Christ is] a stumbling block to Jews and a foolishness to Gentiles, but to those who are called, both Jews and Greeks . . . the wisdom of God" (1 Corinthians 1:23, 24).

20. The separation of theology and science is strongly emphasized today by J. Fischer, among others. His answer to the question, "Can theology make the world as creation understandable to scientific reason?" is a clear "no" (*Freiburger Zeitschrift für Philosophie und Theologie* 41, 1994, p. 491).

21. P. W. Atkins has especially strongly emphasized in *The Creation* (Oxford: W. H. Freeman & Co., 1981) that the concept of God in view of the explanatory power in science is superfluous. Also Stephen Hawking asks, "[If the universe did not have a beginning or had a fully explainable one], where would there still be room for a creator?" in *A Brief History of Time* (London: Bantam, 1988), p. 179.

22. Among the many books about creation theology I have found of particular interest the recent works by J. Moltmann, *God in Creation: A New Theology of Creation and the Spirit of God* (San Francisco: Harper & Row, 1985); W. Pannenberg, *An Introduction to Systematic Theology* (Grand Rapids, Mich.: Eerdmans, 1991); Ch. Link, *Schöpfung. Schöpfungstheologie angesichts der Herausforderungen des 20. Jahrhunderts* (Gütersloh: Güntersloher Verlagshaus, 1991).

23. "It is through wonder that men now begin and originally began science; wondering in the first place at obvious perplexities, and then by gradual progression raising questions about the greater matters too, e.g. about the changes of the Moon and of the Sun, about the stars and about the origin of the universe." Aristotle, *Metaphysics* I ii, p. 9.

24. Amazement is not coercive. Steven Weinberg writes in the final chapter of his book, *The First Three Minutes* (New York: Basic Books, 1977), p. 154: "The more the universe seems comprehensible, the more it also seems pointless."

25. At the absolute zero point of minus 273 degrees Centigrade, there is no heat energy present in gas. Therefore this is the lowest possible temperature.

26. A quantum theory is necessary for the description of microphysical processes as established in 1900 by Max Planck. It was extended to a mathematically consistent quantum mechanics in 1925 by N. Bohr, W. Heisenberg, and E. Schrödinger. A detailed, generally understandable introduction to quantum mechanics can be found, for example, in H. R. Pagels' *Cosmic Code* (New York: Penguin, 1994).

27. Niels Bohr is said to have remarked: "Anyone who is not shocked by quantum theory, has not understood it."

28. Werner Heisenberg writes in *Der Teil und das Ganze* (Munich: Piper, 1969), p. 326: "Quantum theory is . . . a wonderful example of the fact that one can understand a concept with complete clarity, yet at the same time realize that one can only speak of it in images and parables."

29. E. Schrödinger thought up a clever thought experiment in 1935, with which he wanted to show the apparent craziness of quantum mechanics. R. Penrose published a modern edition, in *The Emperor's New Mind* (Oxford: Oxford University Press, 1989), p. 290; easier to read is the version of H. R. Pagels in *Cosmic Code* (New York: Penguin, 1994).

30. According to the modern picture of the structure of matter, the entire universe consists of quarks and leptons. From both families of particles, six kinds and their antiparticles are known, that is a total of 24 elementary particles. In addition, there are the field quanta of the forces which mediate interactions among the particles. This view is hardly final but is more likely to be complemented than completely refuted in the future.

31. Quarks are named after the shadowy creatures in the novel *Finnegan's Wake* by James Joyce. Quarks cannot exist in today's universe as single particles. Two quarks are necessary for a meson and three for a hadron.

32. From C. F. v. Weizsäcker, *Zum Weltbild der Physik*, 6th ed. (Stuttgart: Hirzel, 1954), p. 20.

33. The idea of the origin of the universe from a quantum fluctuation was suggested in 1973 by E. P. Tryon in *Nature*, 246, p. 396. A generally understandable introduction to the topic may be found in A. H. Guth's *The Inflationary Universe* (Reading, Mass.: Addison-Wesley, 1997).

34. Stephen Hawking, for example, speaks allegorically of "God's plan" In *A Brief History of Time* (London: Bantam, 1988), p. 218.

35. Proposed by J. P. Ostriker and P. J. Steinhardt in *Nature* 377 (1995), p. 600.

36. The discoverer of the carbon resonance, Fred Hoyle, writes: "I do not believe that any scientist who examined the evidence would fail to draw the inference that the laws of nuclear physics have been deliberately designed with regard to the consequences they produce inside the stars."

37. B. Carter, in *Confrontation of Cosmological Theory with Observational Data*, ed. M. S. Longair (Dordrecht: Reidel, 1974), p. 291.

38. In scholastic philosophy, the effecting cause (*causa efficiens*) was differentiated from the purposeful cause (*causa finalis*). It was already clear to the medieval philosophers that they do not mutually exclude one another.

39. Exodus 3:1–4:18.

40. Modern philosophers are also concerned with death. Martin Heidegger qualified the human existence as a "being to death," and Karl Jaspers writes: "Life becomes deeper, existence surer in the face of death," in *Philosophie* Vol. 2 (1932), p. 227.

41. Mark 4:3–8 NSRV.

42. Entropy is a term of thermodynamics that measures the degree of disorder of a system or, equivalently, the information needed to describe its actual state. Entropy can never decrease in a closed system.

43. The subject of self-organization will be further discussed in Part 4.

44. It is often assumed that superclusters, clusters of galaxies, and stars formed in that order, the largest structures forming first. This is what the "top-down model" postulates. However, the "bottom-up model" in reverse order cannot be ruled out on the basis of present observations.

45. Systems which are initially far from equilibrium often enter a phase in which they stabilize after a certain period of time. In that state they may oscillate regularly or simply become stationary. One terms this preliminary end state of development an attractor.

46. Paul emphasizes the interlacing of past, present, and future in the Easter

event. In his view, the future is already opening up in the present at Easter, a present that is still dominated by the old (cf. S. Vollenweider, in *Theologische Zeitschrift* 44, 1988, p. 97).

47. For example, J. Moltmann, *The Crucified God: the Cross of Christ as the Foundation and Criticism of Christian Theology* (New York: Harper & Row, 1974).

48. The fatherly proximity of God has been emphasized as one of the central themes in the preaching of Jesus by G. Ebeling, *The Nature of Faith* (London: Collins, 1966).

49. Augustine (354–430 A.D.) remarked about the logic of the idea of God: *Si comprehendis non est deus* (If you understand it, it is not God.)

50. Vivid and horrifying examples are reported by A. R. Damasio, *Descartes' Error: Emotion, Reason, and the Human Brain* (New York: Putnam, 1994).

51. John Bell derived an inequality that must be valid if hidden parameters exist. Experiments in the 1980s demonstrated that these inequalities are broken and that uncertainty therefore is genuine.

52. The word "gas" for airlike substance is an adaptation from the Greek word *chaos* by the Belgian chemist J. B. v. Helmont (1577–1644). In the Flemish pronunciation, the "g" of "gas" is spoken like a voiced "ch."

53. The concept of self-organization has been introduced among many others by M. Eigen, *Self-Organization of Matter and the Evolution of Biological Macromolecules* (in *Naturwissenschaften* 58 1971, pp. 465–523); E. Jantsch, *Design for Evolution: Self-Organization and Planning in the Life of Human Systems* (New York: Baziller, 1975); and G. Nicolis and I. Prigogine, *Self-Organization in Nonequilibrium Systems: From Dissipative Structures to Order Through Fluctuations* (New York: Wiley-Interscience, 1977).

54. B. Hinrichs, *Ich bin*, Stuttgarter Bibel Studien 133 (1988), p. 94.

55. The religious and historical background of John's Gospel are summarized, e.g., in *The New Jerome Biblical Commentary*, ed. R. E. Brown et al. (Englewood Cliffs, N.J.: Prentice-Hall, 1990).

56. For the origin of the name of the Hebrew God, see B. W. Anderson, *Understanding the Old Testament*, 4th ed. (Englewood Cliffs, N. J.: Prentice-Hall, 1986).

57. "In the beginning was the Word, and the Word was with God, and the Word was God. . . . All things came into being through him, and without him not one thing came into being" (John 1: 1, 3 NSRV).

58. "Although doors were shut, Jesus came and stood among them and said, 'Peace be with you' " (John 20:26 NSRV).

59. Metaphors are central elements of theological language, as for example H. Weder emphasizes in *Neutestamentliche Hermeneutik* (TVZ, 1988).

60. The scientific pattern for "the formation of newness" cannot establish Christian hope, but can make hope understandable by supplying relevant metaphors.

61. In 1 Corinthians 15:12–19, Paul expressly describes the resurrection of Christ as the basis for Christian hope.

INDEX